HAUNTED HOTELS OF THE CALIFORNIA GOLD COUNTRY

HAUNTED
HOTELS OF THE
CALIFORNIA
GOLD COUNTRY

NANCY K. WILLIAMS

Haunted
America

Published by Haunted America
A Division of The History Press
Charleston, SC 29403
www.historypress.net

Copyright © 2014 by Nancy K. Williams
All rights reserved

Front cover: Sonora Inn, Sonora, California. *Wendy Williams.*
Back cover, inset: National Hotel, Nevada City, California. *Wendy Williams. Back cover, lower*:
Hotel Leger, Mokelumne Hill, California. *Calaveras County Historical Society.*

First published 2014

Manufactured in the United States

ISBN 978.1.62619.438.0

Library of Congress CIP data applied for.

This book is a promise kept.
It is dedicated to the memory of Jack C. Williams, my best friend.

A special "thank you" to my granddaughters:
Amanda: A dedicated ghost hunter, who's tireless and can walk miles
around lakes, over hills and through museums.
Ashlynne: For funny songs, wishes on a star and rockin' to Neil Diamond
and the Stones.

CONTENTS

ACKNOWLEDGEMENTS

This book is the fulfillment of a promise that was made many years ago. I've always been fascinated with the Gold Country, its history and human stories. My husband and I loved exploring it, and we mastered metal detecting and reading old maps. Our kids learned to pan for gold and treasured vintage bits of crockery and square nails as much as chocolate and chewing gum. Writing magazine articles about our Mother Lode adventures led to thoughts of a book, but it was always postponed. Then my husband became ill, and time ran out. My last promise to him was that I'd finally write that book.

The years passed, and the book nagged now and then like a chronic toothache—one I avoided doing anything about. One day, I realized it had been twenty-six years since I made that promise, and it was time to keep it.

Thank you to my children, who helped me keep that promise: Tom, who kept my tired computer running, for his photographic expertise and many hours of editing, proofreading and handling the technical aspects of putting this book together. Thanks to Wendy for the photographs of the hotels today, memories of fun times and believing that I'd write this book.

Thanks and much appreciation to Aubrie Koenig and Becky LeJeune, commissioning editors, for their patient guidance along the path to keeping this promise.

My thanks to the hotel owners, who allowed us to explore their halls, basements and attics and shared their stories. Thanks to everyone who gave us interviews and talked about their experiences.

Special thanks go to Peter Hertzog, Imperial Hotel, Amador City; Mahmood Ghani, Ione Hotel, Ione; Betty Reid, American River Inn, Georgetown; and Forrest Monk and Sarah Zahn, Hotel Jeffery, Coulterville.

The help of the historians throughout the Gold Country was invaluable. Their thorough research and determination to track down facts and old photographs is most appreciated. These tireless volunteers preserve priceless information about the Gold Country. Thank you to Jim Sneddon and Bill Anning, Tuolumne County Historical Society; Jon McCabe, El Dorado County Historical Society; Pat Chesnut, Nevada County Historical Society; Karen Nicholson and Danielle Ballard, Calaveras County Historical Society.

Many thanks to the paranormal investigators who have shared their findings and conduct their research with honesty and integrity. This book isn't a how-to guide for ghost hunters, and it doesn't discuss the various tools that are so valued by paranormal investigators. There are plenty of other publications that can guide you through the intricacies of the infrared cameras or thermo-imaging and show you how to use an EMF (electromagnetic field) meter or an EVP (electronic voice phenomenon) recorder.

Introduction

Gold was discovered in January 1848, and by 1849, about ninety thousand forty-niners had arrived in California. They headed for the Mother Lode, an area of about two hundred miles extending along the western slopes of the Sierra Nevada. Mexican miners coined the term "La Veta Madre" (the Mother Lode), referring to the incredibly rich vein of gold running through this area. Because there were so many offshoot gold deposits, some as wide as forty-nine feet, this entire gold-rich foothill region became known as the Mother Lode.

By 1855, over 300,000 people were swarming over the hills, burrowing into the ravines, crowding the riverbanks and sloshing about in the creeks, wielding gold pans and shovels. Everyone was looking for gold, but not everyone found it. Disgusted and discouraged, some turned to other enterprises, often opening a store where their first sale was their own prospecting equipment. Shrewd entrepreneurs reaped great profits with their mercantile, shipping and transportation businesses.

Some of the first women came with their husbands and used their ingenuity to earn money, while the men looked for gold. These women cooked meals and took in laundry and sewing. Others saved to open restaurants or boardinghouses. Within a short time, most Mother Lode towns had several boardinghouses, usually owned by women, and the one with the best cook always had a waiting list.

Fine hotels were built throughout the Gold Country to accommodate wealthy visitors and financiers, who expected more lavish accommodations than a miners' boardinghouse. Soon hotels were welcoming railroad tycoons, presidents, rich speculators, merchants, celebrities, con men, card sharks, gamblers and even foreign royalty.

Gold fueled the region's growth, and towns popped up wherever it glinted. When the gold played out, these towns declined or were abandoned. Others were destroyed by fires and rebuilt, only to burn again. Of the 546 gold rush towns, almost 300 have vanished. Some that remain are little more than colorful names on a roadmap. Mother Nature has healed many of the wounds of the mining days, and the Mother Lode is one of the most scenic and historic areas of the United States.

The Golden Chain, Highway 49, winds and meanders through the rolling hills of the Mother Lode. It links charming villages of weathered cottages and intriguing shops with bustling county seats, proud of their gold rush origin. It passes through sleepy mining camps and the deserted remnants of boomtowns, consisting of a few tumbledown buildings with historic markers.

Take time to savor the past and explore the narrow, winding streets. Prowl through antique stores, seeking bargains and pouncing on treasures. If you're inclined, you can sample the best of the region's award-winning wineries and browse through the art galleries and bookstores. At the end of a relaxing day, dine by candlelight on world-class cuisine or grab a seat at an old boardinghouse table, just as miners did over a century ago.

As night falls, snuggle under the down quilts of a Gold Country hotel, meticulously restored to its original Victorian elegance. Or you can opt for a bed at one of the picturesque boardinghouses that were permanent homes for the work-weary men who toiled in the mines.

The Gold Country's long-lived hotels and boardinghouses are full of the flavor and character of centuries past—and maybe a ghost or two. There are many rumors of otherworldly guests and tenants who have stayed on through the centuries, despite remodeling and renovations. There are whispers in empty hallways, unexplained dark shadows, heavy footsteps on the stairs when no one's in sight and wispy apparitions that roam in search of peace that has eluded them for so many years.

Chapter 1
NEVADA CITY

Both Nevada City and its nearby neighbor, Grass Valley, have their roots deep in the Mother Lode, whose sparkling treasure fueled their fantastic growth. Nevada City is a pleasing blend of the old West and Victoriana, nestled among the pine-clad hills. This prosperous, well-preserved little community is dressy, elegant and full of gold rush charm. The entire downtown of this hamlet of around three thousand folks is a National Historic District and the county seat. Its sturdy brick buildings, with their gaily painted iron doors and shutters, are home to many quaint little shops specializing in handmade crafts or wonderful antiques. Its charming cafés offer a variety of tarts, sweet delicacies and Cornish pasties.

A warm summer day is ideal for a stroll down a Nevada City lane, lined with Victorian homes, charming with their fancy gingerbread trim and lace-curtained windows. Colorful, old-fashioned gardens are surrounded by white picket fences or elegant wrought-iron railings. In the fall, Nevada City's winding streets are lined with sugar maples, their colorful leaves blazing like scarlet flames. In winter, its delicate church spires, touched by snowflakes, rise above the forested slopes, creating real-life Christmas card scenes.

Just like the great cities of Rome and San Francisco, Nevada City was built on seven hills, with names appropriate for the times: Piety, Prospect and Lost. There were plenty of other hills, and by 1849, prospectors were erecting tents and shacks on Nabob, Buckeye, Bourbon, Boulder and Oregon Hills.

The small mining camp was first known as "Deer Creek Dry Diggings," but after the unusually snowy winter of 1850, the residents voted in

Nevada, the Spanish word for "snow-covered." The town grew quickly and soon boasted a population of over ten thousand rowdy citizens. When they weren't drinking or fighting, they were busily sloshing about in the creeks, panning for gold. When the easy finds of nuggets and gold dust from shallow placer deposits ran out, they began digging deep into the earth, looking for the rich, wide veins of ore. By 1856, hardrock mining was king here, and Nevada became the third-largest city in California. It was home to the managers and operators of the area's booming gold mines, while the men who worked underground in their tunnels settled in nearby Grass Valley.

As Nevada grew in size and prominence, it suffered a series of seven disastrous fires, which destroyed the town. Each time the citizens rebuilt, they used an ever-increasing amount of brick, leading to the establishment of the Nevada Brick Yard. In 1864, the town underwent its last name change when the western part of the Utah Territory became the state of Nevada. The word "City" was added, and the town became "Nevada City" to distinguish it from the state and to avoid tangled mail at the post office.

Wells Fargo shipped millions of dollars of gold from nearby hardrock mines by stage from the National Hotel, shown here. *Courtesy of Nevada County Historical Society.*

During the mining boom days, Nevada City and neighboring Grass Valley were surrounded by stamp mills that banged away twenty-four hours a day, 364 days a year, crushing rocks to extract the gold ore. Operations closed down only one day a year when the miners gathered with their families for the annual Miners' Picnic.

Nevada City and Grass Valley were surrounded by world-famous gold-producing mines: the Empire, the North Star, the Idaho-Maryland and the Brunswick. From 1850 until they were closed during the 1950s, these mines produced over $300 million worth of gold, making this one of the richest gold-producing areas in the state.

NATIONAL HOTEL

Built in 1856, this hotel complex was composed of three brick buildings, which shared common walls. The National was a classic picture of the Greek Revival style, with a white columned entry and an elegant lobby. It was popular with businessmen, mining investors and speculators, merchants, newspapermen, writers and even a president.

Just two years after the hotel was completed, there was a disastrous fire that started in a storeroom packed full of cigars. The flames completely consumed the building, leaving only a gutted brick shell. It was rebuilt on an even grander scale, with the bricks painted a dark green to contrast with the sparkling white balconies on the second and third floors.

The rebuilt hotel was headquarters for the telegraph office and the Wells Fargo Express, and it was a welcome stop for stagecoach travelers. A gong in the lobby alerted passengers when it was time to board the stage for San Francisco or the Gold Country. The National Alley, which ran along the side of the hotel, led to the stables where the Wells Fargo teams were kept. The stage brought miners and lucky prospectors to town, where some spent their hard-earned gold dust on provisions and gear, but others squandered it at the hotel on whiskey, gambling and girls. Old-timers recall seeing as much as $50,000 in gold coins and gold dust stacked up in the hotel's gaming room.

During the 1864 presidential campaign, the National was the local headquarters for the Lincoln supporters, and four years later in 1868, it served Grant in his bid for the White House. There were plenty of rousing political speeches delivered from the front balcony. Huge bonfires were built in the streets, and citizens carrying flaming torches marched in support of their candidates.

The National Hotel has always been the center of activity in Nevada City. *Wendy Williams.*

Years later in 1905, the National Hotel saw the beginnings of the Pacific Gas and Electric Company, which was destined to become California's largest energy conglomerate. The power brokers and financiers gathered in the second-floor lobby to smoke cigars and sip fine bourbon as they plotted and planned. Ideas flew back and forth like moths, and the air was thick with schemes and smoke. A tiny glimmer of an idea was developing into a bold enterprise that would put millions into their pockets and gas and electricity into the homes and businesses of Nevada City and Grass Valley.

Today, the National is one of the oldest operating hotels west of the Rockies, and some of its early guests have remained through the decades. The odor of cigar smoke is often detected in that second-floor lobby, and today's guests have reported seeing gentlemen in Victorian clothing sitting here, deep in conversation and enjoying their cigars.

GHOSTS

Special events are held at the National Hotel to celebrate the anniversary of California statehood, the Fourth of July and the Victorian Christmas. Everyone dresses in his or her old-fashioned finery and gathers at the hotel for a great time. However, these infrequent gatherings don't explain the strange sights and sounds from times past that remain in the hotel today.

When the National Hotel was investigated by a paranormal group from Sacramento, group members discovered that it hosted a variety of unregistered guests. It's believed a woman was murdered in Room #48 years ago, and several investigators commented on a feeling of heaviness in the air. Room #78, where a young girl died from mumps complications, caused several investigators to have eerie feelings. High EVP readings were obtained in the hotel saloon where a mysterious woman appears and then vanishes quickly. Occasionally, the mystery lady is accompanied by a gentleman in a black frock coat. This same man has also been seen walking up the front steps into the hotel's lobby.

Built in 1856, the National Hotel welcomes travelers just as it did centuries ago. *Wendy Williams.*

Often there's an odor of cigar smoke around the bar, and employees have been frightened by loud, banging noises that move from place to place inside the walls. Plumbing problems have been ruled out, and this noise keeps everyone on edge.

Hotel guests are often alarmed by slamming doors, flickering lights and shadows that appear and disappear around corners or down halls. Overnight guests complain that their doors are opened and closed many times, disturbing their sleep, and deadbolts and door locks are useless. Tinkling, old-fashioned tunes sometimes come from the piano on the second floor when no one is around, and there are plenty of drafts and unexpected cold spots. The Travel Channel program *Ghost Adventures* aired an episode in March 2012 featuring the investigation of the spirits at the National. This group concluded that the hotel has plenty of unseen, spooky guests.

Chapter 2

GRASS VALLEY

The gold rush came of age in Grass Valley, the center of the huge, hardrock gold mining industry. The wealth that resulted was not shared equally as prospectors gave up hope of finding riches in the streams to became company miners, working for a few dollars a day. They spent their paychecks at the company store and rented company houses to shelter their families.

Grass Valley became the richest and most famous gold producing area in California, with a total output of over $300 million. The two largest mines, the North Star and the Empire, produced more than 5.8 million ounces of gold, making their owners and investors fabulously wealthy. These millionaires lived in elegant mansions in San Francisco or fine homes in Nevada City, while the miners and their families were thankful for a comfortable cottage and a vegetable garden in Grass Valley.

The first flakes of gold discovered in 1848 in the American River at Coloma came from placer deposits. *Placer* is a Spanish word meaning "alluvial sand," which is loose sediment or gravel that contains particles of gold. It comes from "lodes," or veins of the ore that's been formed within the rock. Weathering and erosion expose fragments of gold that are washed downstream. Little pockets of the metal accumulate between rocks, around tree roots, in the bedrock, below waterfalls and at the base of steep hills and escarpments. Gold is about nineteen times heavier than water, and panning washes away sand and sediment, leaving small particles, flakes and nuggets at the bottom of the gold pan.

Some areas of the Gold Country had richer placer deposits than others and drew mobs of hopefuls. A few made lucky finds, like George McKnight, who noticed a golden glitter in a rock he was going to throw at a wandering cow. His 1848 discovery brought hordes of gold seekers to the shallow valley, and a rough camp called "Grass Valley" developed quickly.

Very few early gold seekers had experience prospecting. There were farm boys who'd left their mules and plows behind, sailors who'd jumped ship in the San Francisco harbor and clerks who'd abandoned their jobs in stores and offices. They quickly learned the harsh facts about placer gold mining and the hardships of life in the Sierra. Although the riches were immense, finding and extracting gold took hard work and skill. Thousands learned that wading in icy streams, hoping to find a nugget, was bone chilling, often unproductive work. Panning creek sand, shoveling dirt and rocking a sluice box were backbreaking tasks, and many hopefuls spent exhausting hours with little to show for their labors.

Placer deposits around Grass Valley were quickly exhausted, and gold hunting went underground. Fabulously rich veins of gold in the quartz rock were found, but it soon became apparent that big money was needed to wrench this ore from the earth. Once it was mined and brought to the surface, it had to go through several complicated processes before gold could be extracted. Sampling and assay works had to be built, and smelters, refineries and stamp mills were needed. The gold-bearing ore had to be crushed into fine sand, washed in chemical solutions and then extracted. Next, it was formed into heavy bars of bullion for transporting and sale.

Sawmills were needed to process trees into lumber, and water systems had to be constructed to supply power to run the machinery. Specialists were needed to dig the tunnels and shore them up, while engineers supervised all of these complicated operations. Opening a gold mine could cost at least $1 million!

This initial cash investment was supplied by sharp businessmen, bankers and investors, who poured into Grass Valley. They were eager to sink their money into these mining operations, lured by the promise of tremendous wealth. Large corporations were formed to purchase modern mining machinery and hire the stable, experienced workforce that was needed. These miners must know how to gouge and blast deep tunnels through solid rock and methods of extracting tons of gold-bearing ore.

Thousands of Cornish miners, experienced in digging for copper and tin in their native Cornwall, answered the call for men skilled and knowledgeable about hardrock mining. Once a man was hired, he would ask his new employer if he had a job for his "Cousin Jack," a relative back in England. These miners were eager to leave their homeland because the Cornwall mining industry was in a slump, and California held hopes for a new life. Often, mine owners would eagerly put up the money for an additional Cousin Jack's ocean voyage to California. Next, he'd be asked if Jack could bring his "Cousin Jenny," too. Jenny was most likely a wife or sister, since these men wanted their families with them in the United States. At one time, three-fourths of the population of Grass Valley was from Cornwall.

The mine owners' investments in bringing the Cornish miners to Grass Valley quickly paid off. Centuries of work in Cornwall's mines made the Cousin Jacks invaluable because they solved the problems of timbering, blasting, ventilating and handling flooded underground tunnels. Their Cornish pumps sucked the excess water from the tunnels as the men worked twenty-four hours a day. Soon, these grimy-faced miners, burrowing underground, had dug miles of deep tunnels. One mining expert summed

Early photo of Grass Valley with the Holbrooke Hotel on the left. *Courtesy of Nevada County Historical Society.*

up their ability when he wrote, "The Cornish know better than anyone how to break rock, timber bad ground, and how to make the other fellow shovel it, tram it, and hoist it!"

The Cornish miners loved singing and music, and they sang in the mines, at church and in the saloons. They formed brass bands to entertain their friends and families and loudly shouted their enthusiasm for traveling troupes of musicians, singers and actors. They were particularly enamored of the "musical talents" of Lola Montez, who was a newcomer in town. This dark-haired beauty was notorious for her conquests and amorous adventures in Europe. Once described as "a woman of loves, marriages, divorces, adventures," she eventually fled Europe, avoiding a bigamy charge, and embarked on a dancing tour of the West. After performing in San Francisco, she and her troupe headed to the Mother Lode Country, where she took the miners by storm. It was standing room only when the scantily clad Lola twisted and gyrated in her famous "Spider Dance." She wowed the miners, who showed their appreciation by showering her with nuggets and pouches of gold dust.

Deciding to remain in Grass Valley in hopes of snagging a newly rich millionaire, Lola announced that she was taking a leave from her stage career and bought a small house. The worldly courtesan scandalized the town's matrons when she went shopping in low cut, velvet gowns and flirted with shopkeepers, bankers, businessmen and everyone's husbands. Many afternoons, she and her giant pet bear held court, entertaining male guests on the front porch of her home.

Lola was snubbed by most of the town's ladies, but she was befriended by Mary Ann Crabtree, who kept a small boardinghouse. Lola took the Crabtree's young, red-haired daughter, Lotta, under her wing, teaching the precocious six-year-old to dance and sing. Little Lotta bloomed under her mentor's tutelage and became a sensation by the time she was eight. When Lotta took the stage, loud crowds of clapping, stomping miners showered the child with dollars, Mexican pesos and gold. This humble beginning of a fabulous career took little Lotta Crabtree from the crude miners' stages of Grass Valley, Rabbit Creek and Humbug to the great theaters of San Francisco, Paris, London and New York.

When Lola Montez eventually left town, headed for the big time of New York, she was missed by the Cornish miners, who continued to labor in the dark tunnels beneath Grass Valley's streets. Aboveground, in elegant saloons and hotels, the mine owners, investors and shareholders busily counted their profits. By 1856, Grass Valley had swelled into a bustling community of hotels, stores, shops, churches and a school. Over twenty-five thousand folks called the place home, and although there were still plenty of grizzle-faced prospectors hoping to strike it rich, hardrock mining had become the driving force of its vigorous economy.

GRASS VALLEY TODAY

By the late 1800s, Grass Valley's population had increased to about 85 percent Cornish, whose influence and heritage is present today. The annual Cornish Christmas brings crowds of people to town to celebrate and enjoy the street fair and the carols of the Cornish Choir. Main Street still retains many gold rush relics, and the crooked, narrow streets lead visitors past trim little houses that were once the homes of Cornish miners.

This area is home to Cornish pasties, delicious creations of meat and vegetables tucked into a flaky pastry crust. Pasties were a staple in the tin lunch buckets that the Cornish miners carried into the tunnels. Today's visitors flock to local shops well known for their creations, whose recipes date back over 125 years to the Cornish Jennies.

Grass Valley never underwent the boom and bust cycles that are common to so many gold rush communities. This long-term stability is evident today in its prosperous businesses and well-kept neighborhoods, and the town combines its robust past with a bustling commercial present. Grass Valley is an old town experiencing youthful growth, like an aged dowager dressed up in today's trendy fashion.

HOLBROOKE HOTEL

The dark green columns and wrought-iron balcony of this fieldstone building give the Holbrooke Hotel an elegant Southern Colonial appearance. On the list of California Historical Landmarks, it's been impeccably restored and reflects the opulence of the late nineteenth century. Its history is closely tied to its Golden Gate Saloon, built in 1852. This vintage watering hole claims to be the oldest continuously operating saloon west of the Mississippi. An adjoining one-story structure was added at the rear of the saloon and dubbed the Exchange Hotel because of its proximity to the bustling Grass Valley Gold Exchange. The saloon burned in the disastrous fire of 1855, along with most of the other structures in town. This fire convinced the townspeople of the value of using the more fire-resistant brick and fieldstone when they rebuilt more than three hundred buildings.

The Golden Gate Saloon was rebuilt, and in 1862, a second Exchange Hotel was established. It was fortified against fire with heavy, iron doors, and the roof was topped with a twelve-inch-thick layer of brick and dirt. The saloon eventually became part of the hotel, and it has been in operation ever since.

In 1879, the hotel was sold to D.P. Holbrooke, who changed the name from the Exchange to the Holbrooke. After Daniel Holbrooke died in 1884, his wife, Ellen, continued to manage the business until 1908. Then there's a lengthy gap in the ownership history, but in 1971, Arletta Douglas, a longtime Grass Valley resident, rescued it. She was working on a community project to beautify downtown and, after inspecting the old, rundown hotel, pronounced it the "hidden treasure of Main Street" and eagerly sought restoration help from local citizens. By 1982, all the guest rooms had been restored, and the adjacent, historic Purcell House had been acquired, providing eleven additional rooms. The hotel is now owned by Ian and Susan Garfinkel.

During Grass Valley's boom days, the Holbrooke was a favorite stopover for the gold barons, mining magnates, gamblers, presidents and adventurers. President Ulysses S. Grant slept here, as did Presidents Benjamin Harrison and the doomed James Garfield. The old hotel register displayed in the lobby bears the signatures of president-to-be Grover Cleveland, as well as boxers "Gentleman" Jim Corbett and Robert Fitzsimmons. The opera singer Emma Nevada stayed here, as did singing star Lotta Crabtree.

The saloon's ornate, mahogany bar was hand carved in Italy and made the long ocean journey around Cape Horn to San Francisco. It was hauled by wagon 150 miles to Grass Valley, where it was welcomed by the town's imbibing citizens. The Golden Gate was a popular watering hole, and the notorious Lola Montez often dropped by for a nip and to entertain "her boys." Writers Jack London, Mark Twain and Bret Harte enjoyed a drink or two at the bar as they told jokes and spun their yarns.

Over the years, the elegant hotel hosted glittering social events for the newly rich mining moguls and their elaborately gowned wives. Named a California Historic Landmark, it was featured on a September 2013 episode of the Travel Channel program *Hotel Impossible*. Crews painted and gave a new shine to the mahogany woodwork, copper clad walls and Italian alabaster. Now the hotel welcomes visitors just as it did over 150 years ago.

The newly renovated Holbrooke is one of the oldest hotels west of the Mississippi River. *Wendy Williams.*

GHOSTS

Like many other old places, the Holbrooke has guests who have stayed on—and on. Local ghost tour guide Mark Lyon, a Nevada City resident, has done a great deal of historical research, even going door to door in neighborhoods, asking residents about their ghostly experiences. He concluded that there are ghosts in over half of Grass Valley's buildings, including the Holbrooke. Lyon said some noisy revelers of evenings long past still hang out in an old speakeasy in the Golden Gate Saloon. Wedding receptions and special events held in the dining room often have an extra guest, a ghostly gentleman in a black top hat. He's usually seated at a table in the restaurant, reading the newspaper, and occasionally, he's joined by a friend. This spirit suddenly materializes and then, just as quickly, disappears. Those who've noticed him often say, "But he was just there. Now he's gone!"

Because of its reputation for unexplained paranormal activity, it's not uncommon to see ghost hunters waving around EMF meters, taking EVP readings and snapping photos in the halls of the Holbrooke Hotel. A Sacramento-based group of paranormal investigators visited the Holbrooke recently and, after obtaining EVP recordings and countless pictures of orbs, concluded that it is definitely haunted.

Guests and employees have described a woman in a nineteenth-century gown who's seen walking through the upstairs halls. Others have glimpsed an attractive woman with long blonde hair, wearing an elegant gown, who appears and then quickly vanishes, sometimes right through a closed door. The swish of silk is often heard, and occasionally, perfume lingers in the air. Another woman in a flowery dress has been seen upstairs and in the kitchen, while a woman in a Victorian maid's uniform drifts about. Guests and staff say they feel like they're being watched when they're upstairs, and several felt a light touch when no one was nearby. "It just made the hair on my arms stand straight up!" commented a housekeeper.

Room #9 is believed to have some otherworldly guests from time to time. It was once called the Black Bart Room because the Gentleman Bandit occasionally stopped over at the Holbrooke. Unexplained strange noises come from the empty room, and occasionally, a well-dressed, shadowy older gentleman has been seen nearby. A gambler, John Henry Martin, might have made #9 his permanent home when the hotel was his headquarters during the freewheeling days of Prohibition. One evening after dressing for another night of cards and poker, Martin was overwhelmed by melancholy and despair. Defeated by waves of black depression, he cut his throat with his own shaving knife. Hours later, when he failed to appear for his card game, someone went to his room and found the poor man dead, lying in a pool of blood. He left behind a farewell letter, which is now at the Doris Foley Historical Research Library in Grass Valley. Occasionally, this luckless man's image is seen standing at the hotel window. The tragic story of John Henry Martin, "The Suicide Gambler," was featured in 2010 on *My Ghost Story* on the A&E Biography Channel.

One group of paranormal investigators spent two nights in the hotel, inquiring into ghostly activity in the Purcell Annex, as well as the Holbrooke. Group members recorded many high meter readings with sudden spikes and fluctuations, and several members heard noises that sounded like children jumping on the beds in Rooms #20 and #21. Both rooms were vacant at the time. The investigators experienced sudden battery drains, unusual temperature changes, cold spots and chill drafts. Before retiring for the night, they met in Room #1 to compare their findings. They had a voice recorder turned on during their meeting and found that it had captured even more EVPs. These investigators concluded that both the Holbrooke Hotel and the Purcell House "are haunted by intelligent spirits, many of which are interactive and appear to be aware of the investigators' presence."

Some guests and employees have seen the ghost of a cowboy, known as Charlie. He's quite a dandy, decked out in finery that's more commonly worn by twentieth-century cowboys. He's usually seen downstairs near the Iron Door, the basement bar. Occasionally, when Mark Lyon brings a ghost tour group through the hotel, he catches a glimpse of Charlie leaning against the bar, keeping an eye on things.

Young children have spotted Elizabeth, a little girl who appears suddenly and then disappears just as quickly. It's believed that she once lived in the hotel and died here sometime in the early twentieth century. Youngsters' voices and childish laughter have been heard throughout the hotel, most commonly on the lobby stairs leading to the second floor.

The Holbrooke Hotel once had a manager named Edgar, who is still on the job. He has set a record for longtime employment since he was first placed on the company payroll over a century ago. Edgar's been seen now and then in the lobby and the bar, and he's often present when there are important events at the hotel, which are attended by large groups of people. It's rumored that Edgar once got into some kind of trouble here during Prohibition. Whatever the difficulty, he somehow managed to keep his job, and he's still handling his responsibilities today.

Edgar is often blamed for the minor disturbances that are created by balking kitchen appliances and problems at the front desk. When all the hotel's television sets turn off simultaneously, there's a familiar refrain, "It must be Edgar!" When room doors slam loudly, the lights flicker on and off and there are aggravations with the phones, the faithful, long-serving desk clerk gets the blame.

The Holbrooke Hotel has seen plenty of gambling, drinking, gunfights and brawls. It's been the scene of both tragedies and triumphs, and it's little wonder that some players from the past are still here. The present-day hotel manager confirms the presence of ghosts but insists that that they are all friendly spirits, saying, "We've never had any bad ones, and no one ever gets hurt!"

Chapter 3

GEORGETOWN

This small, weathered hamlet was called the "Pride of the Mountains" and once rivaled Placerville as the area's social and cultural center. In 1849, miners from Oregon found many large gold nuggets in the creek, which they named after their home state. They were joined by a company of sailors turned gold hunters, who were led by George Phipps. The ragtag community of shanties and tents that sprang up was dubbed "Growlersburg." This unusual name came from the noise the heavy gold nuggets, called "growlers," made when they rolled around in the miners' gold pans.

In 1852, Growlersburg was destroyed by a fire caused by a photographer taking a picture of a dead man in a gambling den. His flash powder ignited a tent, and the rest was history. The camp was moved uphill to the town's present site, and rebuilding began. Main Street was one hundred feet wide, making it more difficult for flames to leap across. The adjacent side streets were at least sixty feet wide, and most of the new buildings were brick and stone.

The settlement's name was changed to "Georgetown" in honor of George Phipps, and this seemed to bring good luck. More gold was found, and stories of fabulous nuggets and rich lode deposits drew investors, bankers, merchants and businessmen, fueling the area's growth. By 1855, Georgetown boasted a school, a church, a theater, a town hall and a Masonic Lodge, as well as a Sons of Temperance Hall, three hotels, many stores and businesses. The stage line was extended over the mountains, making regular stops at the Georgetown Hotel, which was built around 1849. The local theater presented the latest in classical drama, as well as traveling musical stars, including Lola Montez and Lotta Crabtree, who drew huge enthusiastic crowds.

The population swelled to around five thousand people, and Main Street was lined with locust trees, which sheltered its many brick and stone shops. Nestled along the side streets, there were neat clapboard houses with flower and vegetable gardens, remarkable for their varieties of blossoms, shrubs and fruits. The soil here was rich, not only in mineral wealth but also in nutrients, and gardens thrived. Many plants seen today are offspring of stock obtained from a pioneer nursery started here in the 1860s by a native of Scotland. Some rare and beautiful plants have survived to this day in the old gardens and the pioneer cemetery. Others, like the Scotch broom, which originally came from this nursery, have grown wild over the hills, beautifying the countryside with their golden blooms.

Deep gold quartz mines, like the Woodside, produced millions of dollars in gold, and when their ore started declining, seam mining began. This is a process of extracting gold quartz interspersed with slate, which was found in seams that varied from several feet in width to one as thin as a knife blade. Many smaller camps popped up around Georgetown, and they thrived until the 1930s, when much of the gold was exhausted.

GEORGETOWN TODAY

When the mines closed, many people left Georgetown, while others turned to lumbering in the nearby forests and raising fresh produce. Today, Georgetown is a tiny spot, a bit off the beaten track. It is the gateway to the wild and beautiful Rubicon River country. The nearby American River challenges rafters to brave its boiling rapids and hidden rocks for some white-water thrills. The historical significance of this northeastern-most town in the Mother Lode was recognized when the entire community was made a California State Historic Landmark.

GEORGETOWN HOTEL

After George Phipps threw open its doors on August 7, 1849, the Georgetown Hotel and its bar quickly became the center of activity, and it has remained that way for over 160 years. The large frame structure drew miners, engineers, businessmen and travelers, who came through on the Wells Fargo stage. The hotel's rooms were always full, and the cook was busily dishing up meals in the restaurant. The saloon served lucky prospectors, as well as those down on their luck, rugged cowboys, roughnecks and rowdies, who gathered there to celebrate a lucky find or to drown their miseries.

The first hotel went up in flames in 1852, but Phipps rebuilt, only to have it destroyed by the fire of 1856. The hotel was damaged a third time by flames in 1896. Rebuilt again, portions of the first building were incorporated into the present structure. It's believed that these sections of the hotel date back to 1849.

Today, just as in the past, the bar is a popular watering hole, and it has changed very little over the years. In May 2012, its loyal followers were irate when the California Department of Fish and Game raided the bar and seized its stuffed wolverine. The snarling beast, wearing a red ball cap and clenching a cigarette between its sharp teeth, has been prominently displayed behind the bar for at least fifty years. Citing a law that the wolverine was an endangered species and illegal to possess, the Fish and Game guys whisked the critter away.

While they were at it, these agents also grabbed a stuffed red-tailed hawk. The incident made the news and even a page in *Outdoor Life*, a respected national hunting and fishing magazine. There was such an uproar that Georgetown's representative to the state senate promised to look into the matter. The bartender summed up the current situation, saying, "It leaves a hole in my heart."

GHOSTS

Although the wolverine was rounded up and hauled off, there are plenty of other unusual guests at the Georgetown Hotel who aren't shy about making their presence known. One ghost that often appears is believed to be a former owner, who may have died in the 1896 fire. This spirit has been described as a tall man with gray hair who is wearing 1890s clothing and usually has a pipe clenched between his teeth. He's been encountered on the stairs, in the bar and in the kitchen, where he often stands with his hands on his hips, watching the cook at work. It's believed he's responsible for locking the kitchen door behind the cook, the only late-night employee, when he dares to step outside for a breath of air.

Overnight, after the hotel is locked and the employees have gone home, mysterious things happen, especially in the kitchen. The pots and

The Georgetown Hotel survived several destructive fires. *Courtesy of El Dorado County Historical Museum.*

pans are rearranged, and trash cans are moved about. Sometimes, the back door, although locked the night before, is found standing wide open in the morning. More than one cook has sought other employment after unexpectedly encountering a scowling spirit in the kitchen or being locked out of the building too many cold nights.

In addition to the watchful observer, there's another spirit named Myrna. A "lady of the evening," she often conducted business at the hotel, usually in Room #5. It's believed that Myrna had an unfortunate accident when a jealous boyfriend, in a fit of rage, threw her off the front balcony. Now and then, the lady returns to her favorite room and closes or opens the room's drapes unexpectedly. Guests' toiletries are moved about, and the bathroom faucets are often turned on and left running.

This hotel has a Room #13, where guests and staff have experienced a great deal of intense paranormal activity. It was combined with Rooms #14 and #15 to make an apartment for the hotel bartender. When questioned about ghostly activity, the bartender told an investigator that the hotel actually felt crowded at times because it had so many ghosts.

The Georgetown Hotel does seem to have an impressive register of mystery guests, who've stayed on over the centuries and make themselves known now and then. The staff has reported doors that slam unexpectedly, cold spots that move about, stubborn lights that go on and off, unexpected noises and footsteps in the night. Rooms #1, #10 and #11 have a great deal of paranormal activity. A regular customer known as Big Bill, who was a practical joker, suffered a fatal heart attack in one of these rooms. It's believed that he returns now and then to play pranks, moving things about, hiding people's shoes and belongings. Guests have been awakened in the night by a knock on the door, but when they crawl out of bed to answer, no one is there. Others complain loudly about a young boy bouncing a ball up and down the halls, night or day.

With its many guests, visible and invisible, the bar at the hotel gets pretty lively when the jukebox is cranked up, and there's loud singing and guitar strumming. When the old cowbell hanging from the barroom ceiling suddenly starts clanking in a regular rhythm, the locals roll their eyes and snicker. The raunchy remarks about the ringing of that bell tip off newbies that this isn't ghostly activity. A jokester suspended this cowbell from a cord that runs through a hole in the ceiling, and it's connected to the bed in the Honeymoon Suite, which is directly over the bar.

This present structure incorporates portions of the original building from 1849. *Wendy Williams.*

AMERICAN RIVER INN

Guests receive a gracious welcome to the American River Inn, a carefully restored B&B that's full of antiques and treasures from days past. It sits near the end of Main Street, where the first structure on this site was a miners' boardinghouse, called the American Hotel. Opened in 1853, its rooms were kept full as throngs of hopeful gold seekers poured into town. They were drawn first by the large nuggets found in the creeks and, later, by the rich seam deposits of the nearby Georgetown Slide. A wide vein of quartz gold was discovered at the Slide, and a lode deposit near town produced a huge nugget that weighed 126 ounces. This fabulous discovery led to the development of the rich Woodside Mine, whose tunnels ran directly under the boardinghouse.

The hotel-boardinghouse was damaged in 1896, when a fire started in the nearby Tahoe Saloon. Blasting powder was often stored in basements, and when the flames reached one of these storage cellars, the dynamite

First known as the American Hotel, this was a boardinghouse for miners. *Courtesy of El Dorado County Historical Museum.*

was ignited. The blast threw bolts of cloth, pieces of iron and kegs of nails hundreds of feet through the air, strafing nearby buildings and killing two bystanders. The American Hotel survived the disaster because the large trees surrounding the building acted as buffers, keeping the flames and flying projectiles away. Ironically, in 1899, a spark from the hotel's own chimney ignited the roof and burned the place to the ground.

It took just three months for the owners to rebuild and complete the Queen Anne–style structure that sits on the corner of Main Street and Orleans today. The soft cream-colored building, with its blue pillars and fancy gingerbread trim, has withstood a century of use by folks who come here to get away from the city's bustle and enjoy the peace of the mountains. The American River Inn exudes old-fashioned charm, with its bright flower gardens, huge old shade trees and ancient ore cars from the Woodside Mine. The welcoming veranda, which wraps around the building, is a great place to relax in a rocking chair and watch Georgetown go by. Inside the inn, there's a cozy parlor, complete with lush velvet drapes, elegant china lamps, overstuffed chairs and a handsome old settee. Guests gather here for afternoon wine and canapés, while listening to the sentimental tunes of the old player piano.

GHOSTS

In the evening, guests might be joined in the parlor by Oscar, an unregistered sojourner from another era, who's rumored to enjoy a bright tune with his evening libations. Oscar was a miner who worked in the dark tunnels of the Woodside Mine. He fell under the spell of a lovely young woman, who practiced the world's oldest profession in Room #5 at this boardinghouse. It was true love, and the couple had many romantic trysts in #5.

Then, one night, after Oscar had a bit too much to drink, he got into a brawl with another customer, who pulled his pistol and shot Oscar dead on the front steps. Oscar had been a favorite around town, always ready to lend a helping hand, a jovial, joking sort of man, and everyone was furious about his demise. The stranger decided to leave town quickly before Oscar's many friends took matters into their own hands.

One night, Oscar's lady love, grieving the loss of the man who had cherished her, could not live with her grief any longer and decided to end it all by jumping from the boardinghouse balcony. She landed near the front steps and died of a broken neck, but wiser souls believe that the poor woman really died of a broken heart.

Today, sobs are sometimes heard near Room #5, but generally this is a happy place, and it is known as the Honeymoon Suite. Lovers staying in the room are sometimes awakened in the night by whispers and giggles as their bed shakes, and their bedcovers may even be yanked off. A lamp often goes on and off unexpectedly, and although it has been checked by an electrician, there's no reason for this continuing phenomenon.

Oscar has been seen by many guests as he enters the room from the balcony, looking a bit grimy, as if he had a hard day in the mine. Sometimes, he strolls about and then jauntily leaves and stands at the head of the stairs. Those who have seen him say that Oscar is a friendly ghost, smiling as he passes through the room. Surprisingly, none of the guests seem terrified of this spirit, and one described him as a "friendly ghost who smiles at lovers as he walks through the rooms as if he belongs there." Many visitors have left interesting notes in the guest book about their experiences with Oscar. One wrote, "The highlight of our stay was a visit from Oscar!" Another said, "We were in our bed when a dirty looking miner walked into the room, smiled at us, and left through the door."

It's been said that Oscar sometimes whispers in the guests' ears, and this experience was actually described by one guest, who wrote, "In the middle of the night, I awoke to a whisper near my pillow. When I sat up, it was gone.

Now the American River Inn, it sits on its original site and is home to Oscar, a lovesick ghost. *Wendy Williams.*

Soon the whispering was back. I heard a man in the background...but it was a woman's voice I heard distinctly." Occasionally, a guest reports seeing a woman dressed in a red nightgown, enjoying a drink and smiling at guests. Many investigators believe this is Oscar's lady love.

The friendly ambience of the American River Inn invites today's guests to enjoy its warm atmosphere and share its comforts with guests from the past.

Chapter 4

COLOMA

This tiny village was once the goal of the first eager prospectors hoping to find their fortunes. Gold was discovered here on January 24, 1848, in the tailrace of a sawmill that was being built by James Marshall. Lumber was needed in the growing agricultural community, New Helvetia, which had been started near the Sacramento River by John Sutter, an ambitious Swiss immigrant. He'd received a land grant of forty-eight thousand acres from the Mexican government, which still controlled this territory. The settlement, soon known as Sutter's Fort, became the destination of westbound immigrant wagon trains.

Marshall had built the sawmill in a small valley on the South Fork of the American River because it had plenty of tall, straight pines, and there was water for power. While digging a tailrace to allow water to flow through the mill, the work crew found several gold nuggets. Realizing the problems this discovery could make, Marshall swore the men to secrecy and rushed out of the hills to alert Sutter.

Aware that the gold discovery could ruin his plans to build an agricultural empire, Sutter tried desperately to keep it a secret. However, his efforts failed, and word leaked out, spreading through California, the nation and the world. Workmen deserted Sutter's Fort, and sailors jumped ship in San Francisco Bay. Farmers from the East abandoned their fields, and storekeepers left their businesses. Half came overland and the others by sea. They were joined by tens of thousands from Europe, South America, Asia and Australia. Soon hordes of hopefuls were swarming over the hills of the Mother Lode country, and the gold rush was on.

Within one year, Cullooma, a quiet Indian village, had swelled to ten thousand people. The Indians were quickly shoved out by eager newcomers, who were busily staking mining claims and panning for gold in the American River. The Indian name was twisted into "Coloma," and the town grew quickly, becoming the center of the new El Dorado County. There were saloons, shops, restaurants and hotels, but the boom did not last after the placer deposits of gold ran out.

By 1851, this small valley was once again quiet, and Coloma was known as the "dullest mining town in the whole country." The county seat was spirited away to nearby young, rambunctious Placerville, where there had been a flurry of rich gold discoveries.

Today, Coloma is a village of old homes tucked away among the trees and a few historic buildings, survivors of the early days, scattered along Main Street. It's all been incorporated into a state park, protected from future development. On quiet fall days, the park recovers from a hectic summer filled with streams of tourists, eager to see the grizzled remnants of Coloma, where the gold rush began.

SIERRA NEVADA HOUSE

The first Sierra Nevada House was built on Coloma's Main Street in 1850, when the town was booming. The hotel welcomed merchants, bankers and investors, all eager to line their pockets with gold. These capitalists attracted gamblers, con men and working girls, eager to cash in on the opportunities.

In 1852, Robert Chalmers, a Scotsman, purchased the hotel and quickly got rid of its bawdyhouse atmosphere, attracting a new clientele. During the 1860s, the hotel hosted lavish cotillion balls and social events with live orchestras and dancing. Main Street was often jammed with the carriages and buggies of citizens, who came from miles around, decked out in satins and feathers, like colorful peacocks.

In 1865, Chalmers passed the operation of the hotel to his two sons so he could undertake a new venture. History is vague about its ownership through the intervening years, and in 1886, it was inherited by Charles Schultze. He had driven supply wagons and worked as a blacksmith and a stonemason in Coloma. Schultze kept the Sierra Nevada House going during the lean periods when gold production in the Coloma Valley declined.

This second Sierra Nevada House was built after fire destroyed the first. It's on the original Main Street site next to the Wells Fargo office. *Courtesy of El Dorado County Historical Museum.*

In 1902, the hotel burned to the ground, but Schultze built a community hall and silent movie theater on the old site. He operated that business until his death in 1921, when his daughter, Daisy, inherited it. In 1925, this building was again leveled by fire.

In 1927, the Sierra Nevada House was rebuilt at a crossroads about one mile north of the newly created Gold Discovery Site State Park. This preserved Coloma's few remaining old buildings, and no new construction was allowed. Old photographs were used when the hotel was built to make it look as much like the original as possible. Now, once again, it welcomes tired travelers, eager for good food and a soft bed.

GHOSTS

If this old hotel had as much business as it reportedly has ghosts, it would always be jumping, just as it was one hundred years ago. The Sierra Nevada

Fire destroyed the second Sierra Nevada House around 1925. New construction was prohibited in the park so the third hotel was built at Highway 49 and Lotus Road. *Wendy Williams.*

House has six guest rooms and several unseen occupants, who have been coming and going for years.

Room #1 is a favorite of Isabella, a lady who once lived here and whose footsteps are occasionally heard on the upstairs balcony. This room is often used by the bridegroom when a wedding is held at the hotel. Once in a

while, the groom has to be moved to another room because Isabella persists in turning up the heat, tying the room curtains in knots, moving the furniture about and frightening the already nervous husband-to-be.

Isabella had definite ideas about furniture arrangements, and it's believed that she was responsible for repeatedly moving a certain nightstand from its place in Room #5 into Room #1. This happened so many times that everyone finally gave up and left the piece of furniture where she wanted it.

Room #4 is another favorite of Isabella, who opens the door at night, fiddles with the lights and rearranges the guests' toiletries. This room has seen plenty of violence, and some vestiges of angry emotion may still remain. A mystery woman once lived here and worked in the hotel's restaurant. Reportedly, she had a fiery temper that exploded when she found her lover in the arms of another woman. There was a terrible fight in which she was forced out of the room onto the balcony, where she was pushed or fell over the railing to her death. This angry spirit still roams the hotel, and sometimes her footsteps are heard late at night on the balcony. Guests have been awakened by crashes against the walls, shouts and the sounds of scuffling.

The door of #4 slams open suddenly now and then, and loud footsteps are heard in the hall when no one's there. Possibly this is the dark spirit of another angry hotel employee named Mark. He had a fierce argument with his girlfriend and is believed to have shot and killed her in this room. Paranormal investigators have picked up a high level of activity here and on the balcony outside the room.

Room #3 has been jokingly called the Bordello Room, and it's believed to have been shared by two ladies of the evening. With its two antique brass beds and touches of flamboyant red, its colorful past is obvious.

The hotel has a very large, beautifully ornate, gold-framed mirror, which has been hanging on the wall for many years. Occasionally, the image of a woman in a lovely nineteenth-century gown has been captured in this mirror, and some believe that she might be Isabella. Others speculate that the unfortunate woman, who fell from the balcony outside Room #4, is making an appearance. Mysterious images and shadows are glimpsed in the mirror's depths now and then, and paranormal investigators have obtained high EMF readings near it.

Employees in the restaurant kitchen are often plagued by a mischievous spirit they call Christopher. This pest hides knives and silverware and is continually moving things about, creating chaos. Someone will ask, "Where's the salt?" The answer usually is, "Christopher's got it!" This hyperactive phantom may be responsible for sending shot glasses spinning across the bar and wine bottles flying from their racks. Bartenders frequently complain that someone unseen is watching and persists in turning off the lights.

Chapter 5

PLACERVILLE

In the summer of 1848, three prospectors scratched out $17,000 in gold from a small dry gulch here in just one week. Word quickly spread, and the rush was on. By late summer, over one thousand men were working the ground at this new camp, called "Dry Diggins." By 1849, the number of Argonauts (gold seekers) had swelled to more than four thousand. Claims had been staked on every gulch and hillside, and a rip-roaring camp of tents, lean-tos, ramshackle shacks, crude cabins and even a few clapboard houses sprawled across the hills.

Along with the miners and merchants, seamen, plenty of crooks, cutthroats, muggers, hoodlums, thieves and murderers came pouring into Dry Diggins. Flashy fandango girls, fast-talking con men and slick gamblers conspired to separate the prospectors from their hard-earned gold dust and nuggets. There were robberies and murders daily, and the crime became so severe that by 1851, the new California legislature passed a bill authorizing the death penalty for thefts of property worth more than $100.

Since there was no organized government or formal law, folks took matters into their own hands. Floggings and hangings became commonplace as the vigilance committee acted quickly and talked about it later. The Hanging Tree, a giant white oak in the Hay Yard on Main Street, got plenty of use, where the rule was "Hang 'em first; try 'em later!" Dry Diggins quickly earned its new name of "Hangtown."

By 1854, Hangtown was California's third-largest city, just behind San Francisco and Sacramento. The growing population brought churches and a temperance league, and when the town was incorporated in 1854, civic pride dictated the more socially acceptable name of "Placerville." Just two years later, in July 1856, it was nearly destroyed by a disastrous fire. Rebuilding began with the more fire-resistant brick and stone.

In 1857, the county seat was moved by the state legislature from Coloma to Placerville. Mining gradually declined, but the town gained new life with the discovery of the fabulously rich silver of Nevada's Comstock Lode. For years, Placerville had been the goal of westbound wagon trains of families and adventurers, who'd made the hazardous journey from the East across the rugged Sierras, following the Emigrant Trail. Now travel direction was reversed, and freight trains headed east, loaded with goods and supplies for the Nevada mines. From 1859 to 1866, the Placerville-Carson Road was the main freight route to the Comstock Lode silver mines. This was the greatest period of freighting and staging by horse-drawn vehicles ever known in this country.

By 1860, the young boys of the short-lived Pony Express were galloping through Placerville with their bags of mail. They carried newspapers and letters from worried families in the East for lonely prospectors and homesick immigrants in California. These westbound daredevils were greeted with shouts as they thundered into town after surviving a hair-raising ride, escaping fierce Indian ambushes, parching desert heat or blinding blizzards. After the turn of the century, their route became U.S. Highway 50, one of the nation's first transcontinental highways.

Hangtown's gold gave several entrepreneurs their start, and they went on to become tycoons in finance, commerce and transportation. John Studebaker made wheelbarrows for the miners, forming the nucleus of a company he started with his brothers to manufacture wagons, buggies and, eventually, automobiles.

Phillip Armour started digging ditches and saved enough money to open a butcher shop. He went on to carve out a place in the U.S. meatpacking industry and become the nation's leading meat supplier.

Levi Strauss, a dry goods dealer from New York, fashioned a bolt of canvas tenting into a pair of tough pants for a miner, using little copper rivets to reinforce the seams. These rugged britches were an immediate hit, and within one year, Strauss had become the biggest pants maker in California. By the end of the nineteenth century, he had a plant in San Francisco and was grossing $1 million a year selling the pants known as "Levis."

Mark Hopkins, one of Hangtown's first merchants, opened a hardware store with Collis Huntington, a traveling salesman. They cornered the

Horace Greeley, while traveling the West, made a speech from the second-floor balcony of the Cary House. *Courtesy of El Dorado County Historical Museum.*

market on shovels and blasting powder, charging the prospectors outrageous prices. They eventually formed a partnership with two other successful merchants, Leland Stanford and Charles Crocker. Known as the "Big Four," they financed a grand scheme to build a transcontinental railroad to unite the East with the West. They became the first great western railroad barons, whose fantastic mansions and extravagant tastes symbolized California's new prosperity, supported by gold.

Mark Twain and Horace Greeley came bouncing into town aboard stagecoaches handled by famed driver Hank Monk. Twain's first success came with a humorous tale, "The Celebrated Jumping Frog of Calaveras County," and he later regaled readers with stories of his adventures in the West. His account of the terrifying stagecoach journey across the Sierras with Hank Monk and his loud laments over the condition of his backside made hilarious reading in his tale of the West, *Roughing It.* Horace Greeley was so thrilled with the sights and opportunities in the West that he frequently exhorted, "Go west, young man! Go west!" in the *New York Tribune,* the newspaper he founded.

PLACERVILLE TODAY

Congested and crowded, Main Street is squeezed onto a long, narrow strip of land sharing the bottom of a steep ravine with meandering Hangtown Creek. This old part of town contains many of the original buildings, and there's a wide variety of shops, just as there was in the old days. Festivals and celebrations, picnics and wine tastings draw locals and tourists to town, and the sidewalks are often jampacked. Today, Main Street is thronged with cars, instead of yesterday's mule-drawn wagons, pack trains, buggies and riders on horseback.

Reminiscent of the town's notorious past is the life-size dummy, clad in Levis and work boots, that swings at the end of a rope above the old Hangman's Tree Saloon. The hanging tree, a large white oak, grew here and saw plenty of vigilante justice handed out. Many years later, the oak died and was cut down, its tree stump buried in the basement of the Hangman's Tree Saloon. Today, the old bar is closed and crumbling, believed to be haunted.

Placerville's fine old homes, surrounded by shaded gardens, are scattered up and down pine-clad slopes, and cottages sit where early settlers pitched their tents or built their cabins. The dusty routes of pack trains and meandering miners' trails around hills, streams and gulches have become Placerville's narrow, steep streets.

Numerous small camps and tiny towns sprang up on the outskirts of Hangtown but most have now faded into oblivion. Only Georgetown and Placerville survived those early days of the gold rush. Today, as in times past, Placerville is the supply and trade center for the surrounding area.

CARY HOUSE

The El Dorado Hotel once stood here, but it was destroyed in 1856 by Placerville's most destructive fire. Just one year later on the same site, the new brick Cary House opened its doors to travelers. It was advertised as a fireproof building, an important feature in those days, and was way ahead of its time with a bathroom on every floor and both hot and cold running water. A grand mahogany staircase led to the luxurious rooms on the upper floors, and an elevator was installed in the lobby for guests who wanted a ride.

Travelers lounged in the luxurious lobby, paneled in rich cherry wood and imported mahogany and chatted with the notorious stage star Lola Montez.

They gathered around the Chickering grand piano as she sang scandalous songs and bawdy ballads. Businessmen, mining engineers and investors often met here to discuss the price of gold over cigars and brandy. Newspapermen gathered in the lobby to trade jokes and witticisms with Mark Twain when he came through. Ulysses S. Grant enjoyed the Cary's hospitality on his trip to California, and Horace Greeley stopped here on his travels through the Gold Country. Everyone gathered to hear the fiery political speech he made from the second-floor balcony.

The stagecoach stopped here to pick up passengers and shipments of gold and dropped off gamblers, con men and ladies of the evening. They enjoyed the lush appointments and mixed with the affluent guests, creating a lively atmosphere. The hotel's Wells Fargo office shipped or received over $90 million in gold and silver bullion from California's Gold Country and Nevada's rich Comstock Lode during the hotel's first ten years. Wells Fargo

The Cary House has welcomed the famous and the infamous since the early days of Hangtown. *Wendy Williams.*

had been formed in 1852 to handle banking and the express business in California. Its stages carried mail, freight, passengers and, most importantly, cash and bullion.

When the mining boom ended, the hotel remained open but changed hands many times. In 1911, it was purchased by the Raffetto family, whose forebears had come from Genoa, Italy, at the height of the gold rush. They demolished the old building in 1915 and used the original bricks to build the new Hotel Placerville. In 1926, they changed the name to the Raffles Hotel. Sold again in the 1970s, the new owners restored the historic landmark to its original elegance and renamed it the Cary House.

GHOSTS

The Cary House has some mysterious guests and employees from another era. One of the most notable spirits is Stan, who was the hotel's desk clerk for years. Ever the romantic, Stan fell in love with the beautiful companion of a local gambler, who often conducted business at the hotel. One night, the lady was holding court in the hotel parlor and enjoying Stan's amorous attentions, when her paramour arrived unexpectedly. The jealous gambler flew into a rage and attacked the clerk. Stan ran for his life, but his pursuer whipped out a pistol and shot the defenseless desk clerk at the foot of the lobby staircase. Bystanders watched in horror as Stan, wounded and bleeding, somehow managed to crawl back to the parlor where he breathed his last, gazing into the grief-stricken face of his lady love. Another story says that the desk clerk met a tragic end when the furious gambling man viciously stabbed him. Whatever the method of his demise, the unfortunate Stan was murdered, and he died near the lobby stairs.

Although Stan cashed in his chips, he didn't give up the ghost. Today, he roams the halls of the Cary House, leaving cold spots and orbs in his wake. Many people have sensed a feeling of sadness near the stairs, while others say there's an unseen presence around that area. Ghost hunters have picked up a great deal of EMF activity, and many digital photos of orbs have been taken nearby.

The Cary House has been visited by numerous paranormal groups and has been featured on several television programs. Many psychics believe there are some forms of ghostly manifestations in the old hotel. The second floor has a lot of paranormal activity, and employees often advise travelers making reservations to avoid it if they want a quiet night.

Guests in Room #201 complain of doorknobs rattling in the night, the sound of a key being jammed into the lock and knocks on the door, but no one's there. There's a persistent lavender fragrance, and personal possessions disappear only to show up in odd places. There are complaints about dogs barking in the halls and cats purring softly when there are no pets in the hotel. Occasionally, there's a loud whistling sound that seems to come from the end of the hall or near the elevator. This elevator is the second-oldest west of the Mississippi, and it rumbles and squeaks up and down at night, with no passengers. Some investigators noticed the aroma of cigar smoke in the elevator, even though this is a "No Smoking" building.

People who are sensitive to the presence of spirits have experienced a feeling of profound sadness in Room #212. This was once the temporary home of Arnold Weidman, his wife and baby daughter. Arnold was a teamster, who supported his family hauling freight for local merchants and businesses. One cold, damp winter, he became ill with influenza, and despite many visits from the town doc and his wife's devoted nursing care, Arnold died in this room. His widow and baby were left alone, with no money or means of support, no relatives and few friends. They disappeared, and their fate is unknown.

There are icy drafts and chill temperatures in Room #212, and guests often insist there's a problem with the heating system. The Travel Channel program *America's Scariest Places* featured an investigation by the El Dorado Paranormal Society. Members noted that this room was unusually cold and recorded a very low temperature with the windows closed. This was a sharp contrast to the cozy temperature in the hall just outside the room.

These investigators captured digital images of orbs in the second-floor hallway and the lobby, which were shown on the television program and can be examined on the Internet. A very large, distinct orb was photographed hovering above the lobby desk. The Gauss meters used by these investigators recorded high levels of electromagnetic energy throughout the hotel, with especially significant readings on the lobby staircase. This group even used copper dousing rods to pinpoint spirit activity on the second and third floors. The rods consistently pointed at certain spots where several digital cameras captured the image of a large orb.

Paranormal experts say Arnold Weidman sometimes joins Stan on his restless walks through the halls of the hotel. After one night there, a nonbelieving skeptic said, "I can say this for the Cary House. There is something definitely going on here! Call it spirit activity, ghosts, whatever—there's something here!"

Chapter 6

AMADOR CITY

Once the tiniest incorporated city in the United States, Amador City looks like a movie set with its weathered, false-fronted stores and shops. These old buildings hug the narrow road that winds through the small settlement, down the hill and across Amador Creek. In 1854, this tiny stream, the town and the county were named after José Amador, a wealthy rancher who mined along this creek in 1848. When rich gold outcroppings were discovered in 1851, a settlement popped up and took José's name.

The first two large mines in this area were the Spring Hill and the Little Amador. By 1853, the town's most productive quartz mine, the Keystone, was operating and eventually produced more than $24 million in gold. This amount would be much higher at today's prices. Amador City soon rivaled Sutter Creek and Jackson as it hummed and bustled, with gold fueling its rapid growth.

In 1878, the nemesis of every mining town—fire—struck, and a huge conflagration destroyed almost every wooden building in the community. Only the front portion of the Amador Hotel and the adjacent Fleehart Building were left standing. When the flames were finally subdued, rebuilding quickly began, using stone and brick. Heavy iron shutters, which could be closed to provide additional fire protection, were installed on the windows and doors. Attics were filled with sand and bricks to smother sparks, and tin roofs protected against flying embers and burning debris. Today, the Amador Whitney Museum is in the Fleehart and Kling Buildings, which look much as they did 130 years ago.

The Imperial Hotel was first a store and then converted into a boardinghouse for eager gold-seekers. *Wendy Williams.*

IMPERIAL HOTEL

In 1879, B. Sanguinetti began construction of the handsome old building that stands today at the curve of Highway 49. The walls at the building's base were twelve bricks thick, and they gradually tapered to four bricks at the roof. Sanguinetti first set up a general store in his building but quickly recognized the town's acute need for a hotel as hordes of people poured into town, needing a place to stay until houses could be built. Sanguinetti converted his store into a hotel and built a boardinghouse next door. Old photos show the brick hotel shaded by three tall elm trees, which were eventually removed to prevent damage to the highway in front of the building.

Sanguinetti prospered over the years, and somewhere along the way, the hotel was dubbed the Imperial. It remained in operation until 1927, when it was closed and boarded up. The building withstood the ravages of weather and the passage of time until 1968, when it was sold, renovated and again became a fully functioning hotel.

The Imperial has had a succession of owners over the years and undergone several renovations. Yet it still retains its original warm, red brick walls and high ceilings, and it has the atmosphere of an old-time Gold Country hotel. Today, there are six guest rooms, each with a private bath, and all are located on the second floor. Rooms #5 and #6 open onto the balcony. This is a great place to sit and enjoy the cool evening breezes and a bird's-eye view of the town. Downstairs in the evening, the old Oasis Bar gets into full swing, and there's a dining room for hungry guests. The courtyard at the side of the building is sheltered by century-old stone walls and is a fine place for dining al fresco.

GHOSTS

Since so many people have come and gone at the Imperial, it's not surprising that some spirits have lingered. Several years before Mary Ann and Jim McCamant purchased the hotel, a ghost hunter was startled when she encountered the full-body apparition of a dusty cowboy in Room #1. It's believed that he met his end in this room, and his spirit occasionally becomes restless. He wanders in the halls, slams doors loudly and tinkers with the light switches while guests become unnerved and complain of being watched. Mary Ann came up with a clever idea to calm this roaming ghost by leaving a shot of whiskey in the room where he met his maker. This nightcap seems to have a calming effect, and journalist psychic Antoinette May even mentioned it in an article she wrote for the *Sierra Lodestar*.

A vintage portrait of a young woman in a long, white dress once hung in the hotel's dining room. Customers commented on the uncanny resemblance between the portrait and the lady who sometimes greeted them. She wore a similar dress and often took dinner orders while chatting with the guests. These same diners were flabbergasted when their real-life waitress appeared at their table, and they learned they'd been visiting with the "White Lady."

Peter, the current bar manager, said that the portrait was eventually removed because it was so old and deteriorated. However, the White Lady still appears now and then in the dining room, her favorite spot. Employees told paranormal investigators that they've sometimes seen a "white mist," while others insist that a shadowy apparition is occasionally glimpsed "crouched down on top of a cabinet."

Employees working in the kitchen have heard footsteps in the dining room when no one was present, and they have noticed sounds as if something is being dragged about in the basement below. Most kitchen workers try to

The ghost of a tough cowboy who met his end here in Room #1 is placated by a nightly shot of whiskey left at the bedside. *Wendy Williams.*

The Imperial Hotel survived fires that destroyed much of Amador City. *Melissa Billups.*

avoid the basement, and when they must enter this dimly lit area, they have a creepy sensation of being watched.

Just beyond the courtyard of the Imperial Hotel lies the old Amador City Cemetery. Ghost hunters can take a short flight of steps that have been cut into the hillside down to this historic resting spot. There are many graves in the old cemetery that are marked with marble headstones. There are historical markers throughout, and they tell tragic stories of many lives lost in the nearby mines. Women were often left widowed with large families, and those who could not afford a marble headstone honored their loved one with a wooden cross or marker. Many of these have been lost to time, and today, there are numerous unmarked graves.

The first burial in this cemetery was in 1851, and the last was in 1892. No longer used, the cemetery was neglected and overrun with brush and weeds. During the 1950s, the city council hired a man to clear out the overgrowth, and instead of using a hoe and muscle power, he decided to burn the weeds. In the process, he set the cemetery on fire. The conflagration cleared out the weeds, but it also destroyed many of the century-old wooden grave markers.

Chapter 7

IONE

Bedbug! What a name for this pretty little town tucked away in a green valley, surrounded by hillsides studded with oak trees. Located at the main junction of roads into the central Gold Country and the rich southern mining district, Bedbug became the supply center for the ambitious Argonauts.

As stores and businesses were quickly built along Main Street, the citizens of Bedbug decided their town needed a more respectable name. A well-read prospector, Thomas Brown, suggested "Ione," the name of the heroine of the then popular novel *The Last Days of Pompeii*. Families were drawn to Ione, and a school was built in 1853, quickly followed by the Methodist Church. A flour mill began operations in 1855, and a general merchandise store, the town's first brick building, was completed. Since it carried a great variety of dry goods, clothing and mining supplies, the store enjoyed a booming business from the day it opened its doors.

The region's fertile soil and balmy climate were ideal for raising fruit and vegetables to supply the neighboring mining camps. The Wells Fargo stage came through town carrying passengers and thousands of dollars in gold bullion from the mines en route to San Francisco. In 1876, Ione's citizens celebrated the nation's centennial and the arrival of the railroad, establishing the town as an important rail and shipping center.

In 1894, the Preston School of Industry, a state reformatory for juveniles, opened with seven youths who were transferred from San Quentin. Known as the Preston Castle, the towering red brick structure was perched on a hill,

The first Ione Hotel burned in 1910. It was rebuilt, becoming the Golden Star of Ione. This building was later destroyed by fire. *Courtesy of California State Library History Room.*

overlooking Ione. For years, it housed youthful offenders until they saw the error of their ways or graduated to adult facilities like Folsom Prison.

The Castle is an imposing example of Romanesque Revival architecture and now sits empty and brooding, as restless spirits roam its overgrown grounds. Its dark, winding corridors are still and ominous, believed to be haunted by several severely disturbed, angry young ghosts. Anna Corbin, a housekeeper, bludgeoned to death by some of "her boys" in the 1950s, still shuffles through the gloomy halls and is occasionally glimpsed in the old kitchen. The forbidding Preston Castle has been featured on *Ghost Hunters*, *The Other Siders* and the Travel Channel's *Ghost Adventures*. It is a California Historical Landmark and is on the National Register of Historic Places.

Ione Hotel

The Ione Hotel thrives on the hubbub of Main Street, just as it did in the past. Powerful horses still go surging by, but now they are concealed under sleek, metal hoods. Some of these modern-day carriages pull up outside and decide to stay a while. The hotel has rooms for guests who are tired, and its restaurant draws plenty of hungry diners.

The Ione Hotel was built in the early 1850s, but its restaurant, bar and fourteen rooms still retain an aura of yesterday. A sweeping mahogany staircase dominates the lobby and takes you upstairs to the guest rooms. The hotel was a regular stop for the stagecoach, and travelers gladly disembarked to enjoy its fine accommodations. It was destroyed by fire in 1910, but when it was rebuilt, it was called the Golden Star of Ione. This building was almost completely demolished by another fire in 1988, just before it was taken over by new owners. Deciding to rebuild, they researched old records, photographs and plans and constructed it according to the original 1850s design and specifications. With painstaking attention to authenticity and details, the rooms were furnished with fine antiques, and the result is a hotel that looks much as it did over 160 years ago.

Ghosts

Because of its paranormal activity, the Ione Hotel is high on the "Must See" list for ghost hunters and psychic researchers. Some of the hotel's guests have never really checked out, preferring to stay on and on through the centuries. News of these unregistered guests brought *Ripley's Believe It or Not!* to the hotel, and it was featured on *It's Incredible*. While filming, the camera crew had some unexpectedly frustrating experiences when the equipment was tampered with by elusive spirits. Shots of scenes were interrupted, leaving everyone in the dark when switches were turned off by mysterious fingers. Lights dimmed unexpectedly, and doors slammed when no one was about. These unexplained disruptions caused delays and numerous retakes.

Channel 10 News, KXTV from Sacramento, did a long-running series called *California Postcard*, featuring interesting places in the state. On October 30, 2010, they re-ran the visit that journalist Jonathan Mumm and photographer Bill Carragher made in 1984. Longtime owner Milly Jones told them about one of her unusual residents named George Williams. He'd lived at the hotel in Room #13 for a long time and had died there years before. An article published on Halloween, October 31, 2007, by the *Amador Ledger Dispatch* commented that a "ladies man named George" had died in a fire in Room #13 but failed to include the date.

When Milly assigned Room #13 to guests, chances were good that they would leave suddenly in the night, spending very little time in bed. Others stayed but complained loudly in the morning that a man came into their room, shook them awake and yelled angrily, "Get out of my bed!" Their descriptions of an older, slightly stooped, gray-haired man certainly fit George—only he'd been dead for years.

George has not moved on, and he still resents strangers spending the night in his room. He has been known to pull the bed covers off, bang about the room, slam the door or rattle the knob persistently. Once, a man awakened to see a ghostly figure standing at his bedside, holding a water pitcher, as if ready to spill its contents on him. He yelled, and the apparition faded, but its disappearance was followed by loud banging in the hall. Although there was no one in sight, the racket persisted off and on throughout the night.

There are several stories about children who perished in fires at this hotel, and research shows that it was damaged by flames in 1884 or 1885, 1910 and again in 1988. It's believed that two small children died in Room #9, possibly in a fire.

A psychic detected the presence of a woman who identified herself as the grandmother of a toddler who'd died in a fire in Room #6. Apparently, the firemen were unable to rescue this child in time, and the grandmother's spirit has been tormented by this tragedy. The psychic's research traced this fire back to 1884, when the grandmother had been a hotel guest.

Several paranormal groups have investigated the Ione Hotel and heard many interesting stories from employees. They have seen shadowy figures in the upstairs hall, heard unexplained whispers and footsteps, and witnessed the lights dimming and flickering for no reason. Employees hear children laughing and playing in guest rooms when no one's there. Made beds are suddenly rumpled, and the rooms are messy when they had been in order for new guests. The chandelier in Room #4 occasionally spins about madly, and the random scent of smoke keeps everyone on edge or looking for the fire extinguisher.

Bartenders have seen glasses fly off the shelves, and one employee said that she occasionally felt something brush by when she was working behind the bar. Two dining room employees saw a mysterious cloud that looked like smoke floating about. When one tried to fan it away, this vapor broke apart and then slowly reassembled itself as they watched. The filmy mass slowly drifted to the side of the dining room and gradually disappeared.

Investigators encounter many camera problems, including drained batteries, shutters that won't click and lenses that refuse to focus. High EVP readings have been obtained throughout the hotel, and digital cameras have captured clear photos of orbs.

Occasionally, a group of investigators and psychics holds a séance at the hotel with some strange results. During a session in Room #13, one group experimented with exercises to determine whether an unseen presence had joined them and could follow instructions. The leader placed a balloon in the middle of the séance circle and asked the entity to move it in various directions. The balloon responded and moved as directed. One person became very uncomfortable during this séance and left the group. She said she heard loud footsteps following closely as she left the room, but when she whirled around, no one was there.

During recent years, a terrible, foul-smelling odor was noticed in the small sitting area at the top of the mahogany staircase. This became so unpleasant that guests avoided the area, and despite the use of air fresheners and various cleaning products, the odor persisted. In desperation after trying every imaginable remedy, owner Mahmood Ghani decided an exorcism of the hotel was necessary. This was successful, and the foul smell disappeared—for a while. Lately, people are again commenting about a faint odor near the top of the stairs. Photos have captured orbs on these steps and along the edge of the upper hallway.

Mahmood said his guests often ask if children are playing behind the hotel where there is a small creek. They have heard young voices and laughter, but

This present structure was rebuilt, following original plans, and now closely resembles the first Ione Hotel. *Wendy Williams.*

these strange occurrences always happen when there are no children staying at the hotel. Room #9, the Honeymoon Suite, is always locked when it's not in use. Yet the clear imprint of a child's hand has been found several times on the screen of the TV set in this room. Whose little hand made those prints?

Another puzzling phenomenon is the Black Rose, a shadowy image of a long stemmed rose that has appeared on the wall of Room #13. Cleaning did not remove the imprint, so Mahmood had the room repainted, thinking that would take care of the problem. After the paint dried, he inspected the wall and was gratified to see the rose was gone. The next day, a check of the area revealed a faint shadow of the flower, so it was touched up with a bit more paint. The room was locked to allow the paint to dry and eliminate any possible tampering. The following day, Mahmood was dismayed to find a partial image of the rose had shown up again. Gradually, the flower returned completely. Since then, the wall has been repainted several times, but the Black Rose reemerges. Why is it here? Why can't it be removed? Is it related to the tragedy of a young woman who committed suicide in this room?

Chapter 8

VOLCANO

Some of the first gold seekers in California were soldiers who'd rushed to join the effort to free the territory from the clutches of Mexico. One party, from the First Regiment of New York Volunteers, commanded by Colonel Jonathan Stevenson, sailed around Cape Horn to California in 1847. The men were eager to participate in the conflict that had started with the California uprising, the Bear Flag Revolt of June 1846.

Stevenson's men had little to do, as this short struggle with Mexico ended quickly. The California Territory was transferred to United States control by the Treaty of Guadalupe Hidalgo on February 2, 1848. Coincidentally, the first flakes of gold were discovered at Sutter's Mill on the American River on January 24, 1848, just a few days before this treaty was signed.

News of the gold discovery in California spread like wildfire. Hundreds headed into the foothills, including Colonel Stevenson, who led a group of his soldiers turned prospectors. They found rich placer deposits in the shallow clay of a ravine near present-day Volcano.

After prospecting a bit, Stevenson and several soldiers went on to Mokelumne Hill, another very rich area, but a few of his men remained behind. These soldiers continued to look for gold and endured a very rough, cold winter. The following spring, a party of Mexican miners found the bodies of two of these soldiers, who'd died sometime during the harsh winter. They buried the men in the deep ravine that came to be called Soldier Gulch.

Early prospectors in this gulch found about $100 a day in gold dust, and one took out $8,000 worth of gold in less than a week. Another prospector found twenty-eight pounds of the bright metal in a single pocket in Soldier Gulch. By 1849, hundreds of hopefuls were pouring into this shallow, bowl-like valley, which the early miners thought was a volcano caldera.

In 1851, the settlement became "Volcano" when it was granted a post office, and its tent stores and shacks were gradually replaced by frame and brick buildings. In April 1852, there were over five thousand people shopping in its eleven stores and three bakeries and living in its three hundred houses, seventeen boardinghouses and three hotels. Volcano had a theater, the circuit court, a Wells Fargo and an Adams Express office to handle the mail and gold shipments. The town's eleven saloons did standing-room-only business twenty-four hours a day.

One young prospector, who came looking for gold when he was just sixteen, changed his focus from shining metal to shining stars. George Madeira built a stone observatory and ordered a telescope from France. The delicate instrument survived the rough overland journey from San Francisco, and after it was installed in 1859, Volcano's citizens were proud of its astronomical observatory, the first in California.

Volcano became a very rich hydraulic mining area. With this process, powerful, high-pressure streams of water were aimed at hillsides, washing away soil, boulders and trees, exposing the gold. This yielded large amounts of wealth, but it caused devastating environmental damage. Streams were clogged with mud and dirt, and rivers flooded, depositing silt on farmlands and washing rich topsoil into San Francisco Bay. Navigation was imperiled, fields were destroyed and lives were lost. This terrible damage brought litigation, resulting in the Sawyer Decision of 1884, the nation's first environmental law.

VOLCANO TODAY

An old photograph of Volcano, taken in 1860, shows the damage that heavy hydraulic mining caused in Soldier Gulch. Once a tree-covered ravine, it had become a vast, gaping gulley, with a few buildings teetering on the edge. By 1867, hydraulic operations were dropping off in Volcano, and since the placer deposits had played out, most of the population moved on to more golden pastures. Technically, Volcano did not become a ghost town because some people stayed through the years. Today, about one hundred folks call it home and continue doing business behind a few old, sagging storefronts. The boarded-up, weathered structures and vacant windows of the ivy-

Volcano's Main Street after the boom days had passed. The St. George Hotel is the balconied building on the left at the end of the street. *Courtesy of California State Library History Room.*

The St. George is the third hotel built on this site after two predecessors were destroyed by flames. *Wendy Williams.*

covered buildings that shamble along Main Street give this little village a thoroughly haunted look.

Volcano is the home of the state's first lending library, as well as the first astronomical observatory. Markers scattered around the tiny hamlet identify old buildings and historic sites, making a ramble through town interesting and informative. The General Store, built in 1852, is the oldest continuously operated store in California, and the Bavarian Brewery has been keeping spirits up since 1856. The old jail was always crammed with miscreants, and local legend says the first occupants were the two men who built it.

Don't miss "Old Abe," a cannon that was smuggled into town in a hearse in 1862 by Union sympathizers. They feared an uprising of the town's Confederate partisans, who were eager to divert its gold to the South. After getting the cannon, the Volcano Blues confronted the Southern sympathizers, the Knights of the Golden Circle. Knowing they were outgunned, the Southerners conceded, and there were no shots fired. It's a good thing, too, because the enthusiastic Union men had overloaded the cannon, and if it had been shot, it probably would have exploded.

St. George Hotel

The old saying "The third time is a charm" worked for the St. George Hotel, which refused to die, despite being burned to the ground at least twice. The first building on this site was the Eureka Hotel, constructed in 1853, one of the bustling young community's six hotels. Like so many structures in those early days, the Eureka was a wooden frame building, and it was completely destroyed by fire. The next hotel built on the same spot was the Empire. It, too, was of wooden construction, and when it exploded in flames, the Volcano hook and ladder crew and the bucket brigade couldn't put out the conflagration. This fire destroyed several neighboring structures, along with the Empire Hotel.

Experience finally prevailed, and the third hotel was built with fourteen-inch-thick walls of bricks to make it more fire-resistant. The owner, B.F. George, hoping for divine protection, christened his establishment the St. George in hopes of "thwarting the demonic Fire Dragon." The hotel opened early in 1864 with newspaper ads describing it as "the new St. George." Old lithographs and vintage postcards show an impressive three-story brick hotel with two balconies running along the front of the building.

Maybe the name has been a lucky charm because the St. George has survived for over 150 years and is on the National Register of Historic Places. It has twelve guest rooms on its second and third floors, and there are additional rooms in the Garden Cottage and an annex built in the 1960s. The old hotel is shaded by tall trees and surrounded by lovely flower gardens, a great place for weddings or parties. The first floor has a comfortable parlor with ten-foot-high ceilings and a welcoming fireplace of native rock. This is a cozy spot to relax or read on damp, chilly days. The Whiskey Flat Saloon was added to the hotel in the 1930s, and drinks have been served at its old, original bar for almost one hundred years. Occasionally in the saloon, coins fly through the air, striking the bartender or patrons. No one ever steps forward and admits to the prank, and everyone always blames the "ghost."

Ghosts

In 2008, the Ghost Rush Conference of members of American Paranormal Investigations was held at this hotel. More than fifty well-known paranormal investigators, writers and media representatives spent two days here. Their electronic devices picked up a lot of high readings on the third floor, and a

Above: Guests and employees have had unsettling encounters with otherworldly spirits here in the Jimtown Room. *Wendy Williams.*

Left: The spirit of a little girl is often seen playing in this hallway or peeking from an upstairs window. *Wendy Williams.*

medium detected several different entities. One was described as an older gentleman, who walked with a cane.

Many people, both guests and employees, have seen a young girl with blonde curls, wearing a white dress, who wanders in the upstairs hall. She's usually seen in the Soldier Gulch guest room. A ghost hunter captured a filmy image that resembles a young girl standing in the doorway, and the hotel manager says this child has been glimpsed in an upstairs window. Many people believe that the spirit of this little girl roams between the St. George and the Volcano Union Inn, about a block away.

Hotel employees report scattered cold spots, chilly drafts and lights that flicker or go out unexpectedly. There are unexplained giggles, whispers and footsteps when no one's around. The housekeeper said that she often found previously made beds unmade, with rumpled, wrinkled linens, even though there had been no guests in the room. Newly made beds often had imprints that looked like someone had just laid down on them. Working in the Jimtown Room often made employees uncomfortable and brought feelings of being watched.

When paranormal investigators interviewed a previous owner, they were told a hotel guest had encountered a spirit, who was identified as Charles Osgood. The owner had researched this name and learned that a Charles Osgood had been among the hotel's first guests, more than a century earlier.

Each room at the St. George has a journal where guests can record their observations and any unusual happenings. Several people noted that they sensed a presence in their room and often felt like they were being watched. Some wrote that they had caught a glimpse of a little girl in a white dress, and one paranormal investigator even captured "sing song" sounds on tape. He speculated that these sounds might have been made by this young spirit singing to herself.

Chapter 9

JACKSON

The rolling hills and shallow ravines around the Jackson region didn't have many rich placer deposits. Instead, water, not gold, was the reason this camp came into existence. Its dependable, freshwater spring was a welcome stop for freighters with their mule teams, travelers and prospectors on their way to the southern Mother Lode. Some supplemented Nature's beverage with much stronger stuff, and their all-night drinking sprees left the place littered with discarded whiskey and wine bottles. There were so many empty flasks and containers tossed around that this became known as "Botilleas Spring" (Bottle Spring).

The first diggings around Botilleas weren't very rich, but as more prospectors came and explored the nearby hills, some fabulous strikes were made. These outstanding finds would eventually become incredibly productive hardrock gold mines. If you were willing to work diligently in those early days, you had a chance to strike it rich. A good example of this was Madame Pantaloons, a woman who dressed as a man, worked like a man and became an inspiration to others. When she arrived in Jackson, instead of taking in laundry, cooking or entertaining in the saloons, she donned men's clothing and headed for the hills. She staked her own claim, labored alongside the men, digging and panning, and saved her gold dust. Before long, she had managed to accumulate more than $100,000. Then she sold her claim for thousands of dollars more and went off to live a much easier life.

By 1849, Botilleas Spring had become a trade and transportation center. Business and commerce brought a mixed population of Italians, Serbians,

Slavs and Mexicans, who mingled with the forty-niners from the East. As the little settlement grew and prospered, its citizens thought their community needed a more dignified name. They decided to call the tiny town "Jackson" in honor of Colonel Alden Jackson, one of its most enthusiastic leaders.

The town grew rapidly, rivaling Mokelumne Hill, and in 1852, it became the Calaveras County seat. A year later, its citizens formed a new county, which they named Amador, in honor of José Amador, a successful rancher and miner. Jackson became its government center. In 1862, much of the town was destroyed by a massive fire. Painful lessons were learned about flimsy, incendiary, wood-frame construction, and the community rebuilt with brick or massive stone blocks.

When the placer gold around Jackson ran out in the 1850s, prospectors focused on finding the deep, gold quartz veins and, in the process, discovered the Mother Lode, the principal source of gold. This long alignment of hardrock gold deposits stretched through the Sierra Nevada from north to south and was 1 to 4 miles wide and about 120 miles long. Some veins branching off were a few thousand feet long.

Several rich gold veins around Jackson were mined until the beginning of World War II. The famous Argonaut and Kennedy mines date back to the 1850s, and they are among the world's deepest mines today. The Argonaut

Built in 1862, the National Hotel was popular with mining tycoons, gold speculators, gamblers, gunmen and good-time gals. *Courtesy of California State Library History Room.*

reached a vertical depth of over 5,570 feet, and its total gold production stands at over $25 million. The Kennedy Mine, which yielded over $45 million, ultimately went 5,912 feet down. Jackson became one of the most durable hardrock mining areas of the Mother Lode.

The U.S. government called a halt to gold mining in 1942 because it was considered nonessential for the war effort. Gold was not a strategic metal like lead, iron, zinc or copper, which were used in the manufacture of weapons and equipment. Surprisingly, shutting down the mines did not wipe out Jackson, whose citizens turned to farming, lumbering and ranching.

Two huge wooden wheels dominate Jackson's horizon and are a result of 1912 laws prohibiting the dumping of silt and mine tailings into streams. Originally, there were four wooden wheels, each fifty-eight feet wide and powered by electricity. They lifted mine waste in buckets and dumped it into high flumes, which carried it to a holding reservoir atop a nearby hill.

When gold mining ceased, the corrugated metal buildings enclosing the wheels were torn down for scrap. Exposed to the elements, two wheels eventually crashed into a ravine and were destroyed. Steps have been taken to protect the two remaining wheels, reminders of Jackson's gold mining heritage, and they are among the most photographed landmarks of the Gold Country.

JACKSON TODAY

Today, Jackson is a mix of old and new. One of the town's most picturesque buildings is the quaint, white Serbian Orthodox Church of St. Sava, which presides over an old but well-kept cemetery. Many of the stone and brick buildings along Main and Court Streets date back to 1862. Built after the huge fire, they house modern offices, shops and businesses but retain much of the flavor of Jackson's early days. Their iron-shuttered windows, sturdy doors and second-story balconies are echoes of the past.

NATIONAL HOTEL

This three-story hotel was built in 1862, on the site of the Louisiana House, which was destroyed by a disastrous fire earlier that year. The National Hotel was under construction during the early days of the Civil War, and sympathies in California were hotly divided. The savvy owners of the new hotel, Messrs. Askey and Evans, were businessmen first, Southerners second, and they wanted to capture their share of the traveling Yankee dollars. So their new establishment was christened the National Hotel, and its doors were thrown open to both Rebs and Yanks.

Askey was an incurable practical joker, and he frequently sent eastern newcomers out to fish for salmon in the creek behind the hotel. In hopes of catching his dinner, many an unsuspecting guest spent hours dangling his line and hook in the creek. In 1880, this creek, swollen by winter rains, swept the National's outhouse and two dozen miscellaneous buildings down a nearby ravine.

The front porch served as the courtroom for the trial of an accused horse thief, who'd supposedly stolen the animal in Jackson. He'd been tracked down and hauled back for trial. The unfortunate man produced a bill of sale for the animal, but the former owners of the horse, the same Messrs. Askey and Evans, proprietors of the hotel, loudly denied its veracity. The verdict was "guilty," and the doomed man was marched off to the town's hanging tree and quickly dispatched to the hereafter.

During the boom days of hardrock mining, the National Hotel entertained the Gold Country's movers and shakers and wealthy financiers from New York and San Francisco, as well as several governors of the Golden State. When they visited California, Presidents Garfield and Hoover signed the hotel register and spent the night. A century later, Will Rogers and King Paul of Yugoslavia were guests.

Jackson developed a reputation as a wild and woolly town, where the illegal booze flowed in its rowdy saloons during Prohibition. Gambling was an open enterprise, and slot machines and card games were everywhere. State legislators flocked here for the nonstop poker games and the ladies who worked evenings. The bordellos did a huge business, and the back roads from Sacramento were always crowded with cars headed for Jackson and a good time.

Jackson was a twenty-four-hour town, and the National Hotel was the center of the action. Conga lines wound their way in and out of the hotel rooms, down the halls and into the bar, where a bucket hung suspended in the air. Everyone tossed their money at the bucket, and the lucky throwers got free drinks. The ones who missed the bucket got nothing, and the bar kept the money.

In 1952, the state clamped the lid on the fun by passing some tough laws closing the "cat houses" and gambling parlors. Now, Jackson did not take this lying down, and its active resistance finally brought in the state's attorney general. The world's attention was focused on the colorful scandals, embarrassing arrests and unsavory court battles that took place in this rambunctious, stubborn Gold Country rebel town. Eventually, the law prevailed. The good times passed, and the slot machines and shady ladies became fading memories.

Over the intervening years, the National enjoyed an occasional revival, and although it never recovered the rowdy splendor of its past, it developed more of an Old West atmosphere. Around 1960, John Wayne and Glenn Ford, who were filming a western movie in Sonora, were invited to share the honor of being grand marshals of the Fourth of July Parade. The pair had a rousing good time as their mounts bucked and pranced down Jackson's narrow streets. Then they dropped by the National's saloon for a drink—or two—which led to a friendly game of poker. This developed into an all-night card game, and by the early hours of the morning, the Duke had lost $43,000 to the local car dealer.

Needing a bit of shut-eye, the two cowboy stars headed up the stairs to catch a few winks in the bridal suite. Imagine the scene when the actor's check bounced, and the local sheriff threatened him with jail. "Make it good

After a $4 million renovation, the elegant National Hotel sparkles as it did in the old days. *Melissa Billups.*

or else!" was the lawman's order. Duke took this threat seriously and, just a few hours later, showed up with cash.

The National Hotel had its ups and downs, and by 2008, this once grand dame resembled an old dowager down on her luck. It sat forlorn and quiet on the corner of Main and Water Streets, boarded up, worn and neglected in its declining years. Occasionally, "For Sale" signs were plastered on its walls.

Then in 2010, the hotel was purchased by Stan Lukowicz and his two sons. They set about spending $4 million renovating the dilapidated old building and restoring it to its past magnificence. This dramatic facelift transformed the National into a luxury boutique hotel, offering a five-star experience to its guests. Its thirty-six rooms are lavishly furnished with antiques, a baby grand tinkles in the lobby just as it did a century ago and its restaurant is earning rave reviews. There's a wine cellar and a tasting room, and the old bar has been brought back to its once elegant standards.

GHOSTS

Remodeling and renovations sometimes disturb ghosts, and it's been a common observation that when changes are made to a spirit's old home, it may become upset and more active. Only time will tell whether this is the case at the National. It doesn't seem very likely that some of the resident ghosts, who've made this their home for the past 150 years, just left with the old, worn-out carpet and threadbare drapes.

A group of paranormal investigators visited the hotel before the renovations began and obtained a number of high EVP readings in Room #47, formerly the Bordello Room. One psychic felt the presence of a little girl following the group through the hotel, while others sensed two children, a young boy and girl who once lived here. This pair played on the stairs, slid down the banister and were joined in their romps by a little fuzzy yapping dog. Hotel employees have seen the youngsters in the second-floor foyer and occasionally in a guest room.

A former hotel owner and an employee were working together when they heard several loud crashes and the sounds of glass breaking. Certain that a valuable piece of old glassware or an antique had been destroyed, they searched for the damage but found nothing. This racket happened several times, making everyone wonder if it was caused by the playful children or their dog.

The National Hotel has been restored to its former sparkle and elegance. *Wendy Williams.*

Before the recent renovations, hotel guests were often pleasantly surprised to be greeted at the front door by a gentleman in formal attire, who bowed and then disappeared. Guests occasionally caught a fleeting glimpse of a lovely woman, in an old-fashioned gown, who slowly faded away as they watched. Two young businessmen, wearing 1920s-era suits, passed through the halls, and their neat appearance sharply contrasted with another group of grimy workmen, who looked like they had a hard day in the mine.

Now and then, an attractive young woman in a brightly colored, flapper-style dress lingers in the bar or wanders through the upstairs halls. It's obvious that she's had a bit too much to drink. The apparition of a gambler, wearing a black coat and white shirt with a string tie, has been seen many times by psychics and guests in the saloon. A grouchy cowboy occasionally appears on the second floor, but he doesn't linger long. Neither does another gent, who drops in and is always upset, swearing, yelling and stomping about. A linen cart often moves around in random circles in the upstairs halls as if it's being pushed about by invisible hands. Laughing and talking is often heard in the hotel's halls when there's never any one in sight, and there are random cold spots and chill drafts.

Five antique mirrors once hung on the walls in the small foyer on the second floor. Sometimes shadowy images of faces would slowly appear in one of the mirrors and then quickly fade away, only to reappear in another. When one investigator tried to capture an image with her digital camera, the shutter malfunctioned, and she was unable to snap the picture. After leaving this area, the camera again worked well. Paranormal experts say that mirrors hung together or in a series often attract spirits. Since these antique mirrors are now hung throughout the hotel, will the phantom images appear again? Photographers have taken many interesting digital photos throughout the National Hotel, capturing several orbs in the saloon and the upstairs halls.

Since the renovations, there has been a lot of paranormal activity on both the second and third floors and Rooms #307, #308 and #311 are among the most active. Room doors that have been left open are suddenly slammed shut when there is no breeze. While the renovation work was underway, a contractor stayed in Room #311, but he wasn't the only guest. He complained of loud noises at night that disturbed his sleep and said that his toiletries were often moved around. When he was working on the second floor directly below his room, he often heard loud footsteps moving about overhead. When his room was checked, no one was ever there.

Is it any wonder ghost hunters are certain that the National Hotel is home to as many as thirty unregistered spooky guests?

Chapter 10

MOKELUMNE HILL

This is a tiny, peaceful shell of one of the largest and most violent towns in the Mother Lode. It boasted fifteen thousand citizens, a French Quarter, a Chinatown and fabulously rich placer deposits of gold. Colonel Jonathan Stevenson and a group of New York Regiment soldiers were the first gold seekers to make a lucky find in the river gravel in 1848. They established a camp, which Stevenson named Mokelumne Hill, taking the name from the Miwok word "people of Mokel." That long moniker was soon shortened to "Mok Hill."

It was a tent and shantytown until 1851 when the first adobe building was completed. As the continuous stream of gold supported growth, makeshift saloons appeared, serving liquor around the clock. New stores sold mining supplies faster than the mule-drawn wagons could haul the goods to the camp. Colonel Stevenson was elected *alcalde*, the traditional Spanish office, which had both administrative and judicial authority in the town. One of his first tasks was to draw up a sorely needed system of mining laws and regulations. Due to the extreme richness of this area, mining claims were limited in size to sixteen square feet, and many of these small parcels of land were sold for exorbitant sums, as high as $20,000 apiece.

Unfortunately, Stevenson lost control of the town, and the new laws were ignored. Claims were "jumped," gunfights and murders were common and the bodies piled up. During a seventeen-week period, at least one man was killed every weekend, and in one week alone, five miners were murdered. Overnight, Mok Hill needed a cemetery for the

Protestants, another for the Catholics and one for the Jews. Mokelumne Hill was known as one of the wildest, roughest and most dangerous places in the diggings.

Racial tensions increased, and there was much animosity between prospectors of different nationalities. The French were especially resented because they had made several rich gold strikes. One of these was on French Hill, and it drew a large number of immigrant prospectors, who built a fort as a barricade against the avaricious Americans. When they hoisted the French flag, the Yankees claimed these foreign miners were defying the U.S. government. After calling for every American to drop their shovels, grab their guns and join the fight, Mokelumne Hill was invaded by angry patriots, and for a while, it looked like there'd be all-out war. Eventually, the French were cowed into submission and driven off their rich claims, an act later described as "outright robbery."

Another incident illustrating the fierce animosity between gold seekers of different nationalities took place in nearby Chili Gulch, where huge gold quartz nuggets were found. This time, Americans were driven from their claims by a large group of Chileans in 1849. The Americans retaliated, and there were several skirmishes, causing an international dispute between Chile and the United States. This imbroglio was finally resolved, but deep seeds of hatred were planted among the prospectors, and relations between the two countries remained tense.

There were two thousand Chinese in town, scratching out a living as cooks, laborers and carpenters. They worked in laundries, saloons and hotels—wherever backbreaking drudgery was required. Some tried mining, but like the other foreigners, they were quickly driven from their claims. When a raging fire wiped out most of the town's shacks and saloons, the American miners mourned most loudly over the loss of the little adobe that was the auction house for unfortunate Chinese slave girls.

The wickedness of Mokelumne Hill attracted dangerous outlaws and criminals. The Mexican bandits, Joaquín Murietta and his buddy, Three Fingered Jack, often stormed into town, spending the wealth they'd grabbed from travelers' pockets on lonely roads or from the treasure boxes of the Wells Fargo stages. They'd drop into the fandango halls, have a spin with the pretty señoritas, toss down a bottle of whiskey and then leap on their horses and dash out of town to pillage and rob again.

Eventually, the lawless element moved on, and Mok Hill became a major town in the central Mother Lode. In April 1852, it was voted in as the Calaveras County seat, despite protests by the losers that there were more

First a tent saloon, this soon became the site of George Leger's dream hotel. *Courtesy of Calaveras County Historical Society.*

votes cast than the actual number of voters. Regardless of these sore losers, it remained the county seat until 1866.

By the 1860s, the gold began to play out, and lucky strikes were only made now and then. Prospectors found less glitter in their sluice boxes and gold pans and left. The town slowly declined, while nearby San Andreas was growing, and in 1866, it became the county seat. Today, San Andreas bustles with a shopping mall and markets, while Mokelumne Hill has shrunk to a few blocks of old, crumbling buildings.

MOKELUMNE HILL TODAY

This tiny town has a strong sense of community, and people take pride in its rugged past. Their willingness to stick together and help one another was evident when the Travel Channel program *Hotel Impossible* arrived to feature the Hotel Leger. Over two hundred volunteers lined up to give the old hotel a much-needed facelift.

Occasionally, the quiet night is shattered by the sounds of a herd of cattle being driven down Main Street. Their passing fills the night with the thunder of hoof beats, mooing and even the clanging of a cowbell. The ghost herd disappears as quickly as it came, but it has caused hotel guests and homeowners to rush to their front windows, only to see nothing—just a quiet, deserted street.

HOTEL LEGER

George Leger (Luh-zhay) came to Mokelumne Hill from Germany in 1851 and set up a beer parlor, only to have it wiped out by fire the following year. Although he'd lost his investment, George recouped quickly and started a hotel, which was a wood-framed tent on the corner of Main Street and Lafayette. Leger, drawing on his French ancestry and trying to make a silk purse out of his rough canvas structure, dubbed it the Hotel de France. He catered to Mok Hill's large French population and did well enough to replace the tent with a one-story building next to the new Calaveras County courthouse.

Leger's first building was destroyed by fire in 1854, but within a year, the bon vivant was back in business. He built a two-story stone structure that he christened the Hotel de Europa, and his business boomed. George, who'd always liked the ladies and was now forty years old, set up housekeeping with a beautiful young wife named Louisa, age twenty-three.

By 1860, the census records show George's family had grown to include two children. Ten years later, there were three children, with the youngest named Louisa after her mother, who had died. The grieving widower lost himself in work and devised even more ambitious plans for his hotel.

In 1874, flames once again destroyed the hotel, but Leger remained undaunted and rebuilt. He bought the vacant courthouse, abandoned when San Andreas became the county seat. This fine stone addition added space for a beautiful ballroom, and when the new Hotel Leger rose phoenix-like from the ashes, George held a grand reopening celebration. People came from miles around, and there were so many guests that their carriages blocked Main Street. A lavish entertainer, Leger set out long tables covered with sparkling linens and every imaginable gourmet dish. Guests enjoyed oysters, lobster and caviar, as well as quail, squab and elegant desserts and pastries. Tall candles glimmered as couples, dressed in their finest, swirled around the ballroom, while champagne flowed freely, and the air was filled with music and laughter.

Handsome George Leger cut a wide swathe with the ladies of Mokelumne Hill, and more than one cuckolded husband or jealous bachelor swore to put him out of business. One day in March 1879, Leger was in his hotel room entertaining a lady when someone knocked on the door. Leger opened it to find himself facing the business end of a pistol. The assailant pulled the trigger, and shot point-blank in the chest, George fell back into the arms of his lover, mortally wounded.

The murderer escaped, and suspicious fingers were pointed at W.H. Adams, Leger's longtime friend and owner of the local stage company. Adams had won a contract with Wells Fargo to carry mail and passengers between Sacramento and Stockton, and he'd borrowed quite a bit of money from Leger to get his business started. While he appreciated the help from his friend, Adams, unfortunately, learned that his beautiful lady love had been sneaking around spending time with George while he was out of town.

There were rumors floating about that Adams, consumed by jealousy, had hired a hit man to get rid of his friend in a murder-for-hire scheme. Once the dirty deed was done, the remorseful Adams was overcome with guilt and regret and led mourners in sad, tearful laments when Leger was laid to rest. In the meantime, the two-timing lady ducked out of town with yet another suitor, and no one was ever arrested for the crime.

GHOSTS

Many believe George Leger has never left his hotel. It wasn't long after his death that stories began to circulate about strange happenings at the Leger, and these stories continue today. Because of the number and the frequency of paranormal events, the Hotel Leger has been featured on the Discovery Channel and the Travel Channel's *Haunted Hotels* series.

Former hotel owner Ron Miller recalled that while making his late-night rounds, he saw the shadow of a man, which appeared to be following him. Spooked, he quickly turned around, but no one was there. The dark shadow stayed with him, and as his nervousness increased, Miller whirled around and said loudly, "Good night, George!" The shadow disappeared. Miller says that he's sure Mokelumne Hill has ghosts and includes Leger in this group, saying, "George walks this town. I've seen him. He looks exactly like his picture on the stairs."

Once when Joyce Miller was showing a guest around the hotel, the woman became quite pale, turned and ran down the stairs and outside.

Returning later, she explained that she'd seen the spectral figure of a man standing directly behind Joyce. He was nodding his head approvingly while she explained the hotel's history.

Miller's young son often played in the upstairs hall, and one day he came down to the desk asking about "that man in Room #7." When he was told the room had not been rented and was empty, the youngster emphatically said, "Oh, yes, there is somebody in there! A man just came out the door and told me to be quiet!" This same Room #7 was the one shared by Leger and his wife, Louisa, and it's believed that she died here during childbirth. This tragedy might account for the moans and cries that are occasionally heard by hotel guests. After being shot, George died in this room.

A guest said when he entered Room #7, he felt the hair on his head stand straight up. Frightened, he fled but later decided that he should really check out the room again. Returning, he took another peek inside and experienced the same unpleasant reaction. The old rocking chair in #7 moves back and forth randomly, and if the door is left standing open, it slams shut. The bed is often found rumpled, as if it were used for a little snooze by someone who's never been seen.

Jane Canty owned the hotel for years and has passed it on to her daughter, Ashley Canty. Jane said a guest in Room #7 complained that she'd had a very restless night because something kept pushing down on her legs. Several people who have stayed here said that their legs were pushed about or touched, and that this was persistent enough to wake them up.

Many hotel guests have spent frantic minutes—even hours—searching for their missing car keys, cellphones and iPads, only to have them reappear later in the exact place where they'd been left originally. One family with two young sons shared their experiences in Room #12 in a letter to Jane. They'd had a quiet night but, while packing their clothes to leave, discovered a boy's shoe was missing. They searched everywhere in the room but could not find the shoe. Finally, the exasperated mom said, "We appreciate your sense of humor, but we really have to go. Would you please give us back that shoe?" The dad turned to look at his wife as if she'd lost her mind, and then he saw the missing shoe right in the middle of the room. He said, "There'd been no shoe there before."

Several guests who have stayed in Room #8 have caught a fleeting reflection of an attractive woman in the room's antique mirror, and her shadowy image has been captured in digital photos. Guests often catch a glimpse of a strange woman in Room #2, and a little boy has been seen playing by the fireplace in Room #3. Housekeepers have complained that the beds in Rooms #10 and #11 are torn up and pillows tossed about after the beds had been made. Guests have heard children giggling in the halls, and mysterious shadows glide down the corridors and move around the rooms. Sometimes, a shadow is seen near a window, and then it just disappears. There's an aroma of aftershave or men's cologne in the air, always when no one is around.

Jane Canty worked at the hotel for over twenty years before buying it and has had several experiences with its otherworldly guests. One night, she'd put the dining room in order after a large event and locked a series of three doors so guests could not enter. When she returned in the morning and unlocked the doors, she was shocked to find the dining room in complete shambles. The tables had been pushed together, and the candles, dishes, silverware and wine glasses had been used. There was no explanation, and everyone swore their innocence. So who had a party that night?

Employees sometimes get unseen help, like the bartender who was cleaning up after a New Year's Eve celebration. Going upstairs, she was surprised to find all the scattered champagne bottles had been collected and lined up neatly outside each room with the party hats from the celebration

The spirit of George Leger still keeps a close watch on activities at his hotel. *Wendy Williams.*

carefully stacked on top. She was the only person working, and the guests had consumed liberal amounts of spirits before falling into bed, so who was her mysterious helper? Another bartender, heading home one night, approached the locked front door with her arms full. She was startled when the front door suddenly flew wide open without anyone's help.

Canty contacted Bay Area Paranormal Investigators to evaluate the strange happenings. Group members were accompanied by a medium, and the team leader, Mark Boccuzzi, said they use "cold, hard science" to evaluate paranormal events. Data was gathered by thousands of dollars' worth of sensitive recorders and infrared cameras. A tri-field meter was used to measure electromagnetic frequencies, while thermometers checked cold spots and compasses determined accurate locations. The medium said she was overwhelmed by a number of impressions, commenting, "So many spirits have memories of this hotel. Imagine 150 years of passion and intrigue." She detected the presence of several drunken men in the courthouse jail and said she could hear them worrying about their fates. She was certain that George Leger often observed the daily hotel activities from his post in the lobby, saying, "He's still keeping an eye on his hotel."

This medium had vivid impressions of the "Gray Lady," whom she described as a timid woman in her thirties, wearing a Victorian dress with lacey cuffs and a frilly apron. A high column of energy was detected on a tri-field meter near this Gray Lady apparition. After the spirit faded away, the EMF meter did not detect any energy. One psychic encountered the apparition of another woman dressed in a long white gown and said this could be the mistress of George Leger.

A group of paranormal investigators from Sacramento spent the night at the hotel and interviewed employees, longtime patrons and guests about their ghostly encounters. This group obtained numerous elevated EMF readings throughout the building. The EVP meter readings were high, and they made recordings of unusual sounds using digital audio equipment and a sound enhancer. These investigators captured orbs on their video cameras and were able to get some digital photos.

The basement of the courthouse annex has been a gloomy place with its old jail cells, barred windows and view of the ancient hanging tree. Some psychics felt the presence of a young boy and said he might have been involved in a tragic event here. A longtime hotel customer once described the air in the basement as "heavy" and said, "I felt a fluttering in my chest." Digital photos taken of her in the basement showed the woman surrounded by orbs, with some even on her clothes and chest.

The Hotel Leger hosted many grand balls and cotillions in Mokelumne Hill. *Calaveras County Historical Society.*

Longtime bookkeeper Toni Dale had a strange experience one night when she headed down to the basement to place her records in the old safe. When she opened the door to the stairwell, she was startled to see that it was filled with colorful balloons. She pushed them aside and descended the stairs to the safe. Shortly after, she headed back up the steps and was surprised to find the stairwell completely empty. The balloons were gone. An explanation for these balloons was never found, and there was no party at the hotel that night.

When plumbing repairs were needed, manager Shana Molotch accompanied the plumber to the old jail dungeon. When he asked if she believed the hotel was haunted, Shana shrugged, replying, "People believe what they want to believe." Suddenly, she was shoved so hard by some unseen force that it propelled her across the room. This was answer enough for the startled plumber, and after that, Shana was more cautious when she was asked about the hotel's ghosts.

Once, a tunnel ran under the street from the courthouse basement to the bank. It was used by Leger and subsequent owners to carry their deposits of gold dust and cash to the bank to thwart robbers. In later years, when a bordello was operated here, the tunnel, which is now sealed off, provided an escape route for husbands who didn't want to be seen. During the recent renovations, this creepy basement area was transformed into a bright, cheerful event center, ideal for wedding receptions. Time will tell if this transformation urged its gloomy inhabitants to move on.

Former hotel manager Cathy Van Bebber, whose grandmother and great-grandmother both worked at the hotel, says she's been told that one of the ghosts is a long-gone relative, who was also a hotel employee. When asked about the Leger's haunted reputation, she answered, "We can't guarantee that you'll see a ghost, but it happens so often that we wouldn't be surprised."

Chapter 11

MURPHYS

This camp was established in 1848 by the Murphy brothers, John and Daniel, who found rich placer deposits. First called "Murphys New Diggings," it eventually became "Murphys." The brothers ran their trading tent and hired 150 Indians to dig and pan for gold. Trading brought in about $400 a day in gold dust, and when added to the gold the Indians found, the brothers left their namesake camp in just one year with over $2 million in gold, millionaires before they reached the age of twenty-five. John went into politics, while Dan parlayed his gold into real estate, acquiring more than three million acres of land.

Murphys had incredibly rich placer deposits, and within the first year, fifty tents, several lean-tos and some frame houses were erected. During the winter, miners took more than $5 million in gold from a single four-acre site. The Wells Fargo office shipped over $15 million in gold over the next ten years. Murphys grew quickly and, at its peak, had over three thousand inhabitants, five hundred houses, two steam-powered sawmills, a bank and innumerable dance halls, saloons and bawdyhouses.

A fifteen-mile-long ditch was dug to bring water from the Stanislaus River to Murphys. Then industrious miners built a two-mile-long flume that was elevated three hundred feet in the air to carry water from a creek to a large gold mine. Fires ravaged the town in 1859, 1874 and again in 1893, but its hardy citizens always rebuilt. When gold became harder to find, prospectors moved on to richer diggings, while Murphys' merchants prospered, shipping supplies over the Sierras to Nevada's Comstock Lode silver mines.

Tourists came to Murphys to see the nearby grove of giant sequoias, the Calaveras Big Trees. Credit for the discovery of this grove goes to A.T. Dowd, from Murphys, who stumbled upon them in 1852 while hunting. For a while, it was believed that they were the only giant trees in California, and during the 1860s and 1870s, hotels were built in nearby Avery and Dorrington to accommodate tourists. James Sperry, who started the Murphys Hotel in 1856, established another hostelry inside the grove of big trees, which operated until it burned in 1943.

MURPHYS TODAY

Murphys is home base for visitors to the Calaveras Big Trees and a great place to sample the region's wines. It's home to two dozen family-owned wineries that welcome visitors year-round for wine tasting and tours. Many award-winning Gold Country wineries have tasting rooms on Main Street. The entire town has been named a California Historical Landmark, and folks can wander in and out of shops in quaint, gold rush–era buildings. A casual stroll down Main Street, sheltered by enormous old trees, takes you past charming Victorian homes with colorful gardens and historic brick buildings.

MURPHYS HOTEL

This is one of California's oldest hotels still in operation. It was opened in August 1856 by James Sperry and John Perry to accommodate visitors to the Calaveras Big Trees. With its thick walls of local rock and windows that were protected by iron shutters, everyone thought it was fireproof. But they were wrong, and the hotel was severely damaged by the fire of 1859, which destroyed much of downtown Murphys.

The hotel was quickly restored and reopened in the spring of 1860, and it was considered one of the finest establishments between San Francisco and Chicago. The hotel has welcomed many celebrities over the years, and the original guest register contains the signatures of Mark Twain, President Ulysses Grant and financiers John Jacob Astor and J.P. Morgan. Charles Bolles (aka Black Bart, the Poet Bandit) sought refuge here, probably planning his next stage holdup, while Horatio Alger and the abolitionist minister Henry Ward Beecher dropped in. Thomas Lipton, founder of the tea empire, spent the night, and such opposites as Susan B. Anthony and John Wayne both laid their heads on the hotel's downy pillows. Daniel Webster, who ran for the presidency three times and was secretary of state twice, lingered here in 1878. That same year, he might have bumped into newspaper magnate William R. Hearst, who was elected to the House of Representatives three times and always stopped at the hotel during his political campaigns.

In 1882, the Murphys Hotel was purchased by C.P. and Frank Mitchler, who renamed it the Mitchler Hotel. The business prospered, and the hotel became a mainstay in the social life of the town. Over subsequent years, ownership passed through several hands, and in 1945, the MacKimens family purchased it and renamed it the Murphys Hotel. The family operated it successfully until 1963, when they sold it to a group of thirty-five investors from Stockton, California. Most were former University of the Pacific students, who had a soft spot in their hearts for the hotel where they had been spending time since 1942. They refurbished and improved the old building and added two modern motel wings, just west of the original structure. In

The hotel built by the Murphy brothers was sold to a man named Mitchler, who changed its name. *Courtesy of Calaveras County Historical Society.*

2003, the hotel was sold to Dorian Faught, a longtime Calaveras County resident, who made additional improvements to retain and enhance the hotel's historic character.

On the National Register of Historic Places, this hostelry is recognized as a splendid public house of its period. The iron window shutters and the bullet-scarred door from Murphys' heydays remain just as they were a century ago. Its award-winning restaurant draws diners from miles around, and the historic saloon is a great place to imbibe, to drink to the past and toast the future.

There are nine guest rooms in the original hotel, plus twenty more in the motel wings, dating to the 1950s and '60s. There are no phones, television, alarm clocks or coffee pots in the nine historic rooms with shared bathrooms and showers. Guests in these original rooms, taking a midnight ramble to the facilities, chance running into Eleanor or one of the other earth-bound spirits who never left this hotel.

GHOSTS

You'd be hard pressed visiting the Murphys area to find a resident who hasn't heard stories of unusual occurrences at the hotel or had a brush with the paranormal on some level. There's a journal in every room for guests to record their spooky encounters and unusual experiences. Hotel manager Roxana McClelland said, "Our guests constantly tell us about strange things that have happened. I've found lights on in rooms and signs that someone has been on a bed, even though no one rented the room, and the door was locked." She says footsteps are often heard in the halls at night, but there's no one around. Guests have been awakened by a feeling that someone had entered their room and was watching them. Employees and guests have caught glimpses of misty figures, and partial apparitions have been seen.

One of the hotel's most active spirits is Eleanor, who was a chambermaid during the 1860s. She fell in love with a miner who boarded in the hotel, and the happy couple made plans to marry. However, the miner wanted to make a lucky strike before marriage so he could provide a fine home for his bride. After pledging his undying love, he bade Eleanor farewell and headed off to find his fortune. Eleanor waited for her lover to return, watching for him, day after day, month after month. The months stretched into years, and Eleanor continued working at the hotel, saying she was afraid her miner wouldn't be able to find her if she left. So she toiled on in the kitchen, the dining room and the front desk.

As the years rolled by, Eleanor grew older, but she never lost hope that her lover would return. When she became seriously ill, she was finally forced to face the fact he was really gone, never to return. Sick, and with her hopes and dreams gone, Eleanor said that she had nothing to live for and simply faded away, broken-hearted, dying during the 1890s.

Shortly after Eleanor's death, strange things began to happen. Employees caught occasional glimpses of a ghostly figure in a mirror that's hanging in the Gold Room. There was mysterious activity in the kitchen, with pots and pans tossed about and objects suddenly flying through the air. A maintenance man working on an appliance was startled when a bunch of coffee beans went whizzing by his head. There was no one else present, so who threw the beans? The chef was alarmed when a saltshaker suddenly came sailing through the air and smashed against the wall, just above his head.

When the dining room was closed at night, it was in perfect order, but the next morning, employees would find the place settings rearranged and

Mitchler eventually sold the business and the new owners renamed it the Murphys Hotel. *Melissa Billups.*

dishes moved around. When the staff came to work around six o'clock in the morning, ghostly footsteps were often heard on the second floor. Some employees believe that Eleanor is still trying to do her part around the hotel and that she occasionally attends staff meetings in the upstairs ballroom. More than once, the room's door has been closed, and then it swings open suddenly, but no one is ever on the threshold.

Eleanor isn't the only spirit that has lingered on at this hotel. There's a mischievous child who likes to play in the front office and lobby. Gift shop merchandise is often moved around, and the hotel's historical displays are tampered with. Doorknobs frequently turn like someone on the other side is playing with them, and door locks are meddled with. One night, the hotel's owner and the desk manager watched the lock on an inner door rattle crazily when no one was touching it. The manager stopped its movement, but the lock soon resumed spinning and jiggling as if someone on the other side was determined to open the door. This happened three times.

One employee said she has often sensed a presence near the front desk and has noticed the smell of tobacco smoke or lilac perfume when nobody is around. She told of a former manager who had a fright when the antique chandelier that hangs nearby began to sway and was soon whirling violently. It suddenly tore loose from the ceiling and crashed to the floor, just missing the manager by five inches.

Several employees said the second floor is "creepy," especially around Room #9, the Thomas Lipton Room. When a group of paranormal investigators visited the hotel, one psychic sensed the presence of a tall, attractive woman and a mustachioed gentleman in the front lobby. Later, she picked up the presence of this same woman in Room #9. Other psychics have detected a man in the room, and several who spent the night became quite uneasy and had feelings of being watched. The swishing sounds of satin and taffeta skirts are often heard in this room and the hall. One curious couple requested Room #9, planning to wait up late to "see Eleanor." By 10:30 p.m., they said they "were so spooked" that they were afraid to spend the night. They checked out quickly, without even asking for a refund.

A fine grand piano, believed to be the second oldest in California, has been moved into the Ulysses S. Grant Historic Suite. This room has an old nineteenth-century coal stove and is furnished with period antiques. Near the Lipton and Grant rooms, several investigators have seen "a partial apparition of trouser-clad legs walking down the well-lit hallway." Some who have encountered this ghost believe that it is Black Bart, the poet stage robber who sometimes stayed in the hotel.

The Murphys Hotel was a popular gathering place for locals during the 1920s. *Courtesy of Calaveras County Historical Society.*

Grand parties and soirees were held in the ballroom when illustrious personages like Ulysses S. Grant, John Astor and J.P. Morgan visited. The champagne flowed freely as celebrants danced all night to the music of a string orchestra and the grand piano. In later days, children played upstairs in this ballroom, which had once been a dormitory for boarders and itinerant travelers. It was filled with bunk beds and referred to as "the corral." Occasionally, children's voices and laughter are heard here.

While investigating the ballroom, named in honor of Mark Twain, the American Paranormal Research Association obtained a spooky recording of a woman's voice demanding, "What do you think you're doing?" While sitting quietly around a table, they heard loud banging and knocks coming from the small kitchen near the ballroom. Heavy footsteps came from a corner of the room, and photographs captured several orbs near the kitchen door.

During preparations for an evening event in the Mark Twain Ballroom, the banquet manager closed the heavy window drapes and left the room briefly. She returned to find the drapes had been torn from their curtain rods and were tossed about the ballroom. Everyone denied responsibility and wondered if Eleanor was throwing things around again.

The Murphys Hotel is home to several guests who have remained behind from past centuries. Photo taken in the 1950s. *Courtesy of Calaveras County Historical Society.*

When the housekeeping staff held a meeting on the first floor, members were disturbed by voices coming from the second floor, possibly the ballroom, even though there were no guests or staff up there. The conversation grew louder, sounding like a man and a woman talking as they approached the top of the stairs. The housekeepers remained quiet, listening, but no one ever came down those stairs, and the voices gradually faded away as the hotel grew very still.

Another morose figure who appears now and then is believed to be an old prospector who somehow "fell off" the hotel's second-floor balcony. He's been seen occasionally in the bar, hunched over his drink, probably brooding over his bad luck.

William "Wild Bill" Holt was a robber who made the Murphys Hotel his headquarters, and his signature can be seen in the old guest register. Holt's last visit to the hotel did not turn out well. As he walked in the door, there was suddenly a burst of gunfire, and several well-aimed bullets struck him in the back and chest. The wounds were fatal, and the outlaw breathed his last in the front doorway. Another story has Wild Bill sitting out front, when he was shot in the head and died on the doorstep. This murder is well documented in historical records, and it's believed Wild Bill's spirit still hangs around.

Chapter 12

DORRINGTON

About six hundred people call Dorrington home. This tiny mountain hamlet sits on an old toll road between Murphys and the Bear Valley Ski Area. It's a summer vacation retreat for visitors to the mountains and Calaveras Big Trees State Park, and it's a winter stopover for skiers.

In 1827, mountain man Jedediah Smith found a route east across the Sierras that parallels today's Highway 4, through what would eventually be known as Ebbetts Pass. Years later in 1841, the first emigrant wagon train from the East, the Bidwell-Bartleson Party, followed Smith's route across the Sierra Nevada into California.

Once gold was discovered at Sutter's Mill in Coloma, prospectors and emigrant parties searched for the quickest route over the Sierras to the gold fields. By 1849, some were following Smith's rough trail across the mountains, through the amazing grove of giant trees to Murphys. By 1851, this trail was identified by John Ebbetts, who'd traveled it with his mule pack teams and a survey group looking for a railway route. Ebbetts was killed in an explosion in 1854, but when maps were made of the region, his name was given to the pass in memoriam. Because of its ruggedness, this road was used mainly as a pack train and freight route until it was improved for emigrant travel. Eventually, eight bridges were constructed, making the road much easier for wagons to navigate. It became known as the Big Tree (singular) Route.

Cold Spring Ranch, named for its restorative, icy spring water, was a welcome rest spot along the emigrant wagon road. John Gardner, who'd come to California from Scotland to find gold, gave up prospecting and built a hotel in 1852 to serve travelers. It eventually became known as Gardner's Station and was a regular stop for stagecoaches.

In 1859, the discovery of silver in Nevada's Comstock Lode spurred the construction of the Big Tree and Carson Valley Turnpike, a toll road that followed Ebbetts's trail over the Sierras. Within ten years, this route was crowded with loaded freight wagons, mule pack trains and stagecoaches headed east to the rich silver mines.

This toll road was operated until 1912, when it became part of the state highway system. Known as the Alpine Highway, sections of the road were eventually widened and smoothed, using mule-drawn metal scrapers, the earliest earth-movers.

There were few towns along this early highway, and in 1902, a post office was proposed for the little community around Cold Spring Ranch. An official name was needed, but the postal service rejected "Gardner's Station" and "Cold Spring Ranch" because they were similar to other names already in use. When John Gardner, the son of Rebecca and John, suggested his mother's maiden name of "Dorrington," it was accepted by the postal service. The little hamlet once again changed its name, and the post office

The Dorrington Hotel looks much as it did when built by John and Rebecca Gardner in 1852. It's believed that Rebecca remains as its protective spirit. *Courtesy of Calaveras County Historical Society.*

served the area until 1919, when it was closed. It was later reopened and operated until 1934, when it was closed permanently.

There were a few silver strikes in this area, but over the years, agriculture, logging and raising cattle became its mainstays. The development of the Bear Valley Ski Area in 1961 provided the impetus to improve and maintain Highway 4. Winter sports and tourism draw many people to the beautiful lakes and mountains of this part of the Central Sierra Nevada.

DORRINGTON HOTEL

In 1850, John Gardner had forsaken prospecting and dreamed of starting a sheep ranch, but he needed land. He found it when he met Barnabus Smith, who'd been awarded a parcel of 160 acres of bounty land from the U.S. government for his service during the War of 1812. Smith sold Gardner the land, which had a freshwater spring where countless emigrants stopped to rest after crossing the Sierra. Gardner welcomed them and named his new home "Cold Spring Ranch."

In 1851, Rebecca Dorrington Gardner made the sea voyage from Scotland to the United States, and then she sailed through the Panama Canal up the California coast to join her husband. The Gardners established their sheep ranch and soon saw the need for another enterprise: a hotel.

Their Cold Spring Ranch Hotel was completed in about a year, and by 1852, it was a welcome stopover for tourists who'd come to see the grove of towering sequoias. It's believed that Teddy Roosevelt visited the Big Trees when he came to Yosemite in 1903, and he urged Americans to protect and preserve these giants for future generations.

Around 1889, John Gardner was elected to represent Calaveras County in the state legislature. His word was as good as his bond, and people believed that "a promise given by John Gardner was never broken." Rebecca was known for her kindness and generosity, and the popular couple was widely respected throughout the area. They had four children, who grew up at the hotel.

When he was seventy-six, John became ill and went to Angel's Camp for medical attention. After a short illness, he died there, and his widow continued operating the hotel until she died in October 1910.

Today, the Dorrington Hotel has been completely remodeled with five queen-sized guest rooms, furnished with fine antiques and brass bedsteads. There are two full baths, one at each end of the hall, and a separate cabin with a hot tub, a large stone fireplace and a small kitchenette. In the summer, the hotel's backyard patio and deck overlook the lush, green Dorrington Meadow, bright with wildflowers.

GHOSTS

There are many stories about Rebecca Gardner, who's believed to still oversee activities at the hotel. It seems natural for Rebecca to linger here in the home that she loved and where she spent over fifty years of her life. Guests claim to have seen a wispy figure on the stairs, and sometimes the shadowy image of a woman has been glimpsed in a second-floor window. Footsteps are heard in the empty halls, and tables and chairs are mysteriously moved about at night.

The hotel was sold in 1977 to Bonnie and Arden Saville, who said that they immediately felt Rebecca's presence. "It wasn't exactly welcoming," Bonnie told well-known psychic Antoinette May when she visited. When they began renovating the hotel, the spirit became more disturbed. They were the first owners to make any changes in the original structure that the Gardners had built back in 1852.

The carpentry had to be done after 10:00 p.m., when the hotel's restaurant closed. Rebecca would tolerate this until about 3:00 a.m., and then Bonnie said, "She would start acting up." Tools disappeared, extension cords were unplugged, the lights flickered on and off and the radio blared and then hissed with static. Doors mysteriously slammed shut, locking people in or out, and there were loud, unexplained crashes and mysterious footsteps. Bonnie observed, "I know that Rebecca didn't like this at all."

Eventually, the renovations were completed, and the Savilles and their three children settled in. They converted the garage of a nearby gas station they had purchased in 1975 into the Lube Room Saloon. They served beer and burgers, and this became the tiny close-knit community's gathering place. The Savilles were finally able to coexist in harmony with Rebecca, and they operated the hotel for twenty-eight years.

In 2006, they sold the Dorrington Hotel to Marc and Dana Lanthier. To celebrate their first holiday season in the hotel, Marc decorated the outside of the building with strings of colorful Christmas lights. Proud of his handiwork, he took some digital photos of the hotel. When he downloaded them on his computer for viewing, one picture of the hotel's exterior was clear and sharp, but the second similar view held a surprise. A vaporous mist swirled around the building, and a phantom-like figure appeared to be floating above it. There was no reasonable explanation for this phenomenon, and Marc ventured the thought that it could be the ghost of Rebecca keeping watch over her beloved home.

During one holiday season, small artificial trees were decorated and placed in each guest room. Every morning, the guests awakened to find their little Christmas trees had been tipped over, and the ornaments scattered around the room. Before nightfall, the trees would be straightened and redecorated. The following morning was a repeat of the previous one, with the trees again upset. No one heard a sound during the night, but guests and employees wondered aloud if this was the work of Rebecca or her children.

The ghost in the old Dorrington Hotel is a protective and watchful spirit. Once, during the night, there was a gas leak in the kitchen, and Rebecca is believed to have awakened the entire household and alerted them to the imminent danger. Everyone escaped safely from the hotel, and repairs were made, but no one forgot that the spirit averted a disaster. Sometimes, hotel guests have awakened in the morning to see a single footprint at their bedside that they were certain had not been there the night before. Was Rebecca making her nightly rounds, checking to see that everyone was safely tucked into their beds?

Owner Marc Lanier contacted a group of paranormal investigators and asked them to explore the possibility of ghosts in the old building. The investigators rented all the rooms and were the hotel's only guests for a weekend. They obtained high EVP readings, and their digital voice recorders picked up sounds they identified as the voices of both men and women, as well as a young child. These paranormal experts didn't capture any visual images with their cameras, but they heard loud footsteps in the upstairs hall and doors slamming during the night. A man's voice was heard outside, but when the investigators looked out the window, no one was there. These paranormal investigators concluded that the Dorrington Hotel is haunted by one or more intelligent spirits.

Chapter 13

COLUMBIA

Gold was found here in March 1850 by Dr. Thomas Hildreth and his brother. This part of the southern Mother Lode was incredibly rich, and within a few months, their tiny camp had exploded into a tent city called Hildreth's Diggings, which grew quickly into a town of several thousand. Prospectors often found gold in the topsoil, and they dug holes as deep as sixty feet and hauled away the dirt. This was screened and run though sluice boxes to wash out the metal, and a very large amount of high-quality gold was recovered. This digging and excavation left a wide expanse of ghost-like, gray boulders and enormous rocks as large as houses scattered around the outskirts of town. It looked like an ancient battlefield where giants had thrown rocks at each other.

Lack of water hindered the mining operations, so in 1851, the Tuolumne County Water Company was formed to dig a ditch to bring water from a creek. Unfortunately, the creek didn't have enough water for mining and also to power a sawmill that was needed to process trees into lumber. The progressive citizens decided to haul in heavy steam equipment to power the sawmill, and soon there was plenty of lumber to build wood-frame houses.

The town site was platted, and its blocks and streets were laid out. Merchants, seeing a business opportunity, came in droves, bringing goods and their wives and children, increasing the population of Hildreth's Diggings to six thousand. Before long, there were 150 stores and shops busily selling goods, supplies and materials in one of the largest towns in California.

The citizens renamed their community "American Camp" and, a short time later, changed its name again to "Columbia, the Queen of the Southern Mines." A post office was established in 1852, and a school and several churches were built. There was a newspaper and over forty saloons and gambling halls for evening relaxation. Then in 1854, fire, the scourge of the mining towns, destroyed everything in Columbia except its one brick building.

When the town was rebuilt, locally made red brick was used, and iron doors and window shutters were installed as fire protection. Additional bricks were laid over the wooden roofs to ward off the burning embers that spread fires so quickly. By 1855, seven cisterns, with a capacity of fourteen thousand gallons of water, were built under the streets, and the local water company was able to pipe water for firefighting, as well as household use. These original water pipes were so durable that they were used until 1950, when the state finally installed a new water system.

In 1857, a second fire destroyed every frame building in the business district, and the flames even burned several new brick buildings. Rebuilding began again, and a volunteer fire department was formed. A hand-pumper fire engine was purchased in San Francisco and hauled hundreds of miles into the Gold Country. This small, bright red pumper was christened "Papeete," and volunteers lined up to become firemen. The following year, a second larger pumper was purchased and was a welcome addition to the fire department. As the volunteers drilled and practiced, tearing through the streets, pulling their pumper engines, the town folk breathed a bit easier.

Columbia's rich gravel deposits were exhausted by 1860, and many people had moved on. During the 1870s and 1880s, there was little business, and neglected, abandoned buildings were torn down. Their foundations were demolished by prospectors, who scoured these sites for gold. The population continued to decline, and by the 1920s, only 599 hardy souls remained. By 1934, the town was a run-down, dilapidated remnant of a once progressive, prosperous community.

Many of the hundreds of settlements that sprang up during the exciting days of the gold rush had succumbed to fire, the elements, vandalism and neglect. Throughout the years, Columbia had retained a rugged, frontier appearance and presented an opportunity to preserve a typical town of this colorful era. In 1945, the legislature passed a bill appropriating $50,000, which was matched by public funds, raising enough money to acquire the land and buildings in the oldest section of town. This became the new Columbia State Historic Park, a memorial to those pioneers, prospectors, entrepreneurs and dreamers who had come west to find their fortunes.

Today, Columbia is a piece of living history, where you can catch a ride on the one-hundred-year-old stagecoach as it rumbles through town. Stroll down Main Street, sheltered by huge trees, and browse through authentically restored shops, the bank, the Wells Fargo Express office, the City Hotel and the Fallon House Theater. In Columbia, you can experience life as it was back in 1855.

GHOSTS

Park employees, shopkeepers and docents are convinced that Columbia has an unseen population of spirits. Carol Biederman, a ghost tour guide and historian, says emphatically that Columbia has a great deal of ghostly activity. Another docent told us about a park aid, Maria, who was certain that she heard someone call her name every evening when she made her rounds. As the shadows gathered, she'd hear, "Maria, Maria!" but no one was there. This incident occurred most evenings while Maria worked in the park.

Another state employee, making her evening rounds after the park had closed, spotted a light in an old store on Main Street. She went to its empty back room to turn off the light and was suddenly startled by a loud, angry voice yelling that women didn't belong in the building. This warning was repeated, and the frightened woman rushed outside. When the building was investigated soon after, the store was empty.

The Columbia Mercantile is home to the spirit of a little girl, who was the owner's daughter. She became ill and died from an unknown fever when she was only seven years old. Now she plays pranks and makes mischief in the back of the store. Occasionally, merchandise tumbles from the shelves, and employees have caught glimpses of a small girl with long, black hair, peeking out from behind the counter.

The two-story brick schoolhouse, built in 1860, had around 368 students. When park aides were setting up a replica of an old classroom, they were surprised when rulers, pencils and paper were moved about at night, and sometimes supplies were even put away. Every time a second-grade reader was left out on one particular desk, the next morning, the aides would find it lying on the floor. Could it be that the student assigned to that desk felt he'd moved on to more advanced reading?

FALLON HOTEL AND THEATER

Owen Fallon, an Irish stonecutter, built a boardinghouse for miners around 1852 and called it the Maine House. It was destroyed in the fire of 1857, but Fallon rebuilt. Two years later in 1859, his frame building burned to the ground again. Finally, Fallon wised up and turned to brick when he rebuilt the boardinghouse for the third time.

Business was good, and in 1863, Fallon expanded and bought the two-story brick building next door. He cut a hole in the wall, connected the two and turned the second floor into a grand ballroom. Next he converted his boardinghouse into a fine hostelry that he called the Fallon Hotel. He planted a lovely rose garden in the back, which was a wonderful place for his guests to walk and enjoy time away from the hustle of Columbia.

In 1885, Fallon's son, James G. Fallon, inherited the hotel and converted the upstairs ballroom into four large suites. Then he built an elegant, new ballroom on the first floor, which was a great success. He added a large, fancy saloon, and once he had the place the way he wanted it, James G. put his establishment on the market. The building sold quickly,

The Fallon Hotel and Theater changed hands many times between 1890 and 1940. It operated briefly as the Columbia House. *Courtesy of Tuolumne County Historical Society.*

and the new owner added a stationery store and coaxed Wells Fargo into setting up shop there.

The Fallon Hotel passed through a number of hands and had several new names until 1944, when it became the property of Robert Burns, the president of the University of the Pacific. When the State Parks system acquired the town of Columbia the following year, Burns sold the old hotel to the state for the grand sum of one dollar. When the restorations were completed, the university set up a summer theater program, and the Fallon Hotel and Theater reopened.

GHOSTS

Thousands of people have passed through the doors of the Fallon Hotel, and some of these guests still linger in its halls. A strong odor of smoke has been picked up in different parts of the hotel, a reminder that this place burned to the ground not once, but twice. Some keen-nosed guests have detected the smell of whiskey here and there, although the saloon was replaced by an ice cream parlor long ago. During this remodeling, a phantom youth was often seen climbing through a back window. When the construction crew rushed inside, there was never anyone around, leading to the conclusion that it was a youthful spirit in search of a sweet treat.

Guests in Room #13 are often startled by a young woman wearing a Victorian gown, who suddenly appears and vanishes just as quickly. Other guests who've heard of this ghost request a different room, only to find that they have been joined by this same spirit, who seems to easily pass through walls.

The ghost of a little boy has been seen in Room #3 and the second-floor hallway. He likes to play and often takes other children's toys and hides them. This spirit has been seen by several psychics. A father, traveling with his toddler son, stayed in this room and the youngster ran about, laughing and playing as if he had an unseen companion. When the child was put to bed, he fought sleep and seemed to watch his little playmate darting about the room.

The furniture is often moved in Rooms #1 and #6, and guests have seen shadowy apparitions in both. There are strange noises and cold spots in the halls and guest rooms. A team of California paranormal experts investigated the Fallon Hotel recently and concluded that it is definitely haunted.

Since the hotel and the Fallon Theater are in the same building, most guests don't take much notice of the mustachioed gentlemen seen occasionally in the upstairs halls. Elegantly dressed in century-old finery, they stroll about and are usually presumed to be actors from a production, but these gents are from another time.

The Fallon Theater, which is part of the hotel complex, has been the scene of some unusual events, and many people swear that its control booth is manned by a spiritual entity. Very high EMF readings have been recorded in this control booth, and some unusual photographs of orbs and shadowy figures have been taken. The wiring has been completely updated, so why do the lights flicker on and off periodically?

The paranormal activity in this theater has been investigated by psychics, and some believe that the restoration work that was done by the state may have upset certain spirits, while causing others to move on. Even when the theater is empty, it is common to hear the buzz of muffled conversations and the rustling sounds typical of an audience waiting for a performance. The ghost of James Fallon has been seen roaming backstage and in the halls of his theater, usually wearing a top hat and a long coat and surrounded by cigar smoke.

CITY HOTEL

The City Hotel was purchased by the State of California in 1947 and underwent a complete renovation in 1975. It sits on the old site of a brick building that held a blacksmith's shop and the Lager Beer Saloon. In 1860, it was converted into a hardware store, and in 1865, owner George Morgan added a frame structure called Morgan's City Hotel. He continued to add on and made space for a bar, a music hall and theater, a restaurant, Cheap John Louis's Auction House and Shine and Company's Stage Line. Columbia's fires damaged Morgan's building complex, but he stubbornly patched the place up and reopened its doors.

George Morgan had a fiery temper and once, in a fit of anger over the theft of a bag of flour from the kitchen, threatened to close his hotel completely. He raged that he wasn't as angry over losing the flour that had cost fifty dollars as he was about having to hike four miles to Sonora to replace it. When Morgan died, his family took over his various businesses and ran them for years, finally selling out in 1911. In 1947, the state purchased the City Hotel to become part of the new state park, and it was completely renovated.

The City Hotel was developed in 1865 by George Morgan, who converted a saloon and blacksmith shop into this building. *Courtesy of Tuolumne County Historical Society.*

GHOSTS

Every room in the City Hotel is decorated in the fashion of a century ago and furnished with fine antiques. The story of the ornately carved bed in Room #1 lends some credibility to the theory that a spirit entity can become attached to an object. In this case, it's the bed. This piece of furniture is a lovely antique that might have been imported from Europe for a San Francisco mansion.

There's speculation that this bed was ordered by a wealthy, young Columbia businessman as a wedding gift for his bride. According to the story, she planned to leave her home in Ohio and make the difficult journey west to join her fiancé. However, she became terribly ill during her journey and died before reaching California. Her grief-stricken groom sent the bed to San Francisco, where it was stored in a warehouse for years. Long after its owner's death, the bed was discovered in storage and was eventually sold to an antique dealer. Sometime later, this same bed reappeared in Room #1 of the City Hotel.

This hotel had not experienced any paranormal activity until this antique arrived. Everyone agrees that after the ornately carved bed was moved into Room #1, strange things began to happen. Doors opened and closed when no one was around, lights flickered on and off and a scent of perfume often wafted through the empty halls. One guest staying in the hotel reported that her young son repeatedly awakened her, saying that he was afraid of a "lady in a white dress standing by my bed."

Guests who tried to get a restful sleep in the bed in Room #1 often complained that they were repeatedly awakened by sobs, loud sighs and choking gasps. Others have been disturbed by the opening and closing of the room's door and mournful sighs. There seems to be a lot of residual sadness attached to this bed or the room. Some paranormal experts believe that the spirit of a young woman, who may have died in the bed, has become attached to it. Others speculate that the room is occupied by the spirit of a woman who died in childbirth. Some ghost hunters suspect that there may be two female ghosts who account for all the activity.

One rainy night, a couple sought shelter in the hotel, and as the only guests, they were given Room #1. Since the place was quiet, they should have had a peaceful night. But this was not to be, and the next morning, they complained that they'd gotten little sleep, saying that they'd been kept awake by the sounds of sobbing and crying.

The hotel staff has become so accustomed to the paranormal activity in this room that they have even named one of the spirits "Elizabeth." During séances and Ouija board sessions at the hotel, sensitives and psychics have formed their own conclusions and agree that one of the spirits in Room #1 is, indeed, named Elizabeth. Some investigators believe that a woman known as Elizabeth did die in childbirth in Room #1 and that her pain and sadness can still be felt here.

Some type of tragedy that involves a baby, grief and sadness does linger within the walls of this old building. One night, the desk clerk was taking towels upstairs to a guest, and as he passed through the parlor, he noted a woman sitting in a corner. She was holding a baby and sobbing as if her heart was broken. When the clerk asked if he could help, he was amazed to see the woman vanish right in front of his eyes.

Carol Biederman, a ghost tour guide, was intrigued by the stories of these paranormal occurrences at the hotel. Her thorough research showed that there had been a brawl in the first-floor saloon, which was directly below #1. Guns were drawn, and shots were fired. Reportedly, a stray bullet went through the saloon's ceiling, penetrating the floor of the second story and

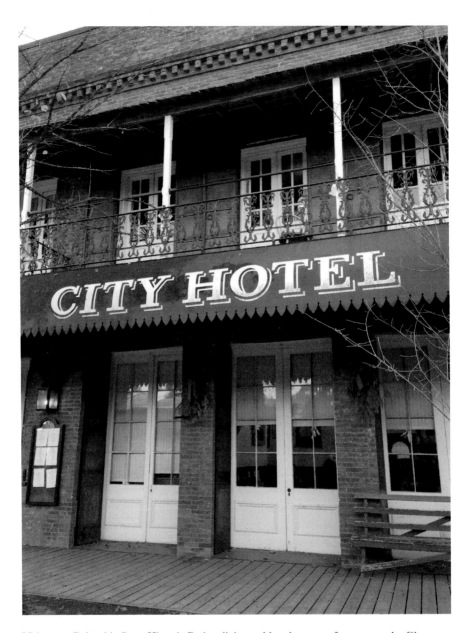

Visitors to Columbia State Historic Park, a living gold rush town, often stop at the City Hotel. *Wendy Williams.*

killing a baby, who was in Room #1. Could such a tragedy have caused the mournful sighs and sounds coming from this room?

Room #6, next to Room #1, has had a lot of paranormal activity. Guests have reported that there is "something weird" in this room and say they've seen the room's doorknob slowly turn back and forth. When the door was thrown open, the hall was empty. After this happens several times, the disturbed guests usually insist on moving to a different room. This part of the second floor of the City Hotel was once a music hall, where there was a lot of activity, causing ghost hunters to speculate that this caused some spiritual holdover.

Guests in Room #10 have complained of being repeatedly shaken awake by unseen hands. Unbelievably, this has happened to some guests several nights in a row. Others have been startled by the shadowy figure of a man on the stairs that psychics think might be George Morgan. Is he making the rounds checking to see that all is well in his hotel-boardinghouse? Poor George came to an unfortunate end. Overcome by despondency, he hanged himself from a beam in the back of the saloon in 1879.

Chapter 14

SONORA

This picturesque Gold Country town is one of the prettiest of the many small hamlets along the Golden Chain Highway. Tucked in among oak and pine-covered hillsides, Sonora reflects 160 years of the area's progress and growth. The town of around five thousand people hums with commerce, just as it did when it was known as "Sonora Camp," back in 1851. Washington Street, the main thoroughfare, was widened and paved after its towering old elms were removed several years ago. It's lined with small retail stores and businesses, whose façades range from Early California Colonial to Retro Fifties style. The heavy iron shutters, designed to protect buildings from fire, have been replaced by sparkling window glass. The numerous boutiques, shops and antique stores are eclectic havens of overlooked treasures and relics of the old days. It's not unusual to find a family heirloom tossed in among today's commercial products and maybe even a gold nugget or two.

Meander down the narrow side streets, shaded by ancient apple trees and tall elms, and you'll find grand, old Victorian- and Queen Anne–style homes. They're surrounded by colorful gardens and spiky, wrought-iron or white picket fences, some leaning with age. Cool, dark walkways lure pedestrians through sturdy, stone buildings with their fortress-like walls, covered with ancient ivy that was planted a century ago.

This was the center of the Southern Mines, with its many rich placer deposits. When coarse nuggets were discovered here in 1848, droves of hopefuls rushed in. Most of these early arrivals were from Mexico and South America, and by the end of 1849, there were over ten thousand Mexicans in Sonora Camp. Tents blossomed like wild flowers on the hillsides, and the night skies were lit up by hundreds of campfires. The rustic settlement quickly mushroomed into a tiny metropolis with a distinctly Latin flavor.

Seemingly overnight, the camp's dirt tracks were transformed into dusty streets, lined with squat adobe buildings, fandango halls, gambling tents and saloons. On Sundays, these narrow streets were nearly impassible, clogged by burly miners, card sharks, gamblers and schemers looking for a good time. There were card games, gambling, drinking in tent saloons, rowdy singing and dancing, with one miner playing the role of a fair maiden dancing partner. There were horse races, battles between captured wild bears and bulls and vicious cock fights, and everyone turned out for the traveling shows featuring musicians, circus and magic acts, vaudeville skits and dancing girls.

Many of the gold seekers were from Sonora, Mexico, and a lot of these immigrants brought their wives and families north. They were followed by other women and children from Peru, Chile and France. The number of foreign women who had come to Sonora actually outnumbered those who came from the East Coast, the Midwest and the Oregon Territory. The town's streets were filled with a polyglot of languages, and the growing settlement took pride in acquiring a bit of polish and refinement. Clotheslines blossomed with dresses and petticoats, a newspaper was published and there was even talk of building a school for the increasing number of children. Sonora became the center of a large number of smaller camps, and it was the place to get supplies, a good meal, decent lodging and a taste of forgotten luxuries like lobster and ice cream.

Sonora was luckier than many gold camps and had only one small fire in 1849, but its good luck ran out in 1852 when the Great Fire burned nearly every building in town. Despite the destruction, its citizens did not give up and set to work widening the streets to make it more difficult for flames to leap from one side to the other. The town was rebuilt, using the more fire-resistant brick and stone. Next, they organized a fire department, and its brave firemen were able to quickly squelch a fire in 1853 and another in 1854.

The gold rush didn't last long in Sonora, and by 1850, the "easy pickins" of gold had been panned from the creeks or scratched from the topsoil. No longer possible to find thousands of dollars of gold in a day, more work was required to gather a few hundred, and that's when the trouble began. As the supply of easy gold decreased, the Yanks insisted they had the right to dominate the region and began shoving foreigners out and seizing their claims.

In 1850, the fledgling legislature of the new state of California passed the Foreign Miners' Tax, requiring all "furriners" to pay $20 a month just to look for gold. In U.S. dollars today, that's the equivalent of $560 per month. This law was primarily aimed at forcing out Latinos, and many balked, refusing to pay the exorbitant tax. Some fled Sonora when the greedy Americanos began organized attacks on the Mexican, Latin American and Chinese immigrants.

These hostilities and the unfair tax brought fierce retaliation from Mexican miners, who turned to guerrilla warfare. Some became outlaws, embracing a life of crime and preying upon the hated Americans. The names of bandits Joaquín Murietta and Three-Fingered Jack struck terror in the hearts of the Anglos as the number of holdups and murders climbed daily. Instead of a bustling center of commerce, Sonora again became a hotbed of lawlessness and constant turmoil. Americans carried guns and Mexicans carried knives because minor disagreements often turned into serious fights and murders.

In July 1850, the frightened Americans banned all foreigners from Tuolumne County. They drove peaceful Mexican families from the area, creating even more trouble and strife. Sonora's population quickly shrank from over ten thousand people to only three thousand souls. Business enterprises failed as shops and stores closed because there were no customers, bringing hard times and dire financial losses to the town's once prosperous families.

In 1851, realizing the grim consequences of their bigoted handling of the Mexican population, the Anglos lowered the Foreign Miners Tax to three or four dollars per month. Sonora never regained its population, and by 1860, two-thirds of the miners had moved on. Eventually, the population stabilized, and Sonora became the business and government center of Tuolumne County.

GUNN HOUSE

The Gunn House, built in 1850, dates back to the early days of Sonora, and it is the town's oldest building. The first two-story adobe, it was built by Lewis Gunn, who'd joined the rush to California in 1849. He'd made the difficult five-month trip overland across Mexico to the Pacific. Then he'd boarded a sailing ship for the journey up the coasts of Mexico and California to San Francisco. Once his feet touched dry land, Gunn headed for the Mother Lode country.

After months of scrambling over the steep hills, prospecting for gold, which he wryly described as just "digging holes," Gunn decided to find another way to make a living. He had a smattering of medical knowledge and some helpful apothecary information, and since there were no physicians in Sonora Camp, he decided that his skills fit the bill.

Gunn began treating the numerous ailments and injuries of prospectors, using common sense and his knowledge of medicines, herbs and first aid. The miners were plagued by dysentery from drinking bad water, and prospecting in the rain and snow was responsible for numerous cases of pneumonia and lung ailments. Scurvy, stiff backs and arthritic legs caused "the misery," and, of course, there were plenty of stabbings and gunfights. The well-liked "Dr. Gunn" did his best, and the survival rate of his patients was much higher than it would have been without his ministrations.

Gunn also assumed the responsibilities of Tuolumne County recorder, and he was kept busy filing the mining claims of lucky fellows who'd found gold. They didn't mind paying him four dollars to make their ownership

The oldest building in Sonora, dating to 1850. Lewis Gunn bought an interest in the *Sonora Herald*, and the building became home to the newspaper and his family. *Courtesy of Tuolumne County Historical Society.*

legal, and this money helped ease Gunn's tight financial situation. He saved his cash diligently, and in November 1850, he bought an interest in the *Sonora Herald*. This was the first newspaper in the Gold Country, and Gunn hired local workers to build an adobe structure to house the operation. The first floor of the building was devoted to the newspaper and the recorder's office. The second story became the living quarters for his family.

Gunn's wife, Elizabeth, and their four children left their Pennsylvania home and headed for California in 1850, making the difficult, eight-month voyage around Cape Horn, landing in San Francisco in August 1851. The family boarded a stage for the rugged trip inland and, when they finally arrived in Sonora, were met by a welcoming crowd, who'd turned out to meet the popular doctor's family.

The Gunns lived in their house ten years and then moved to San Francisco. Their home was sold and converted into a hospital, in use until 1899 or the early 1900s. The building was later purchased by the Bisordi family, who remodeled it into a hotel-boardinghouse. Known as the Rosa Italia Hotel, this name was shortened to the Italia, and it was operated by the family matriarch, Josephine. Her delicious cooking drew hordes of hungry folks to

During the early 1900s, the old Gunn home was operated by the Bisordi family as the Rosa Italia Hotel. *Courtesy of Tuolumne County Historical Society.*

her table, and she never lacked boarders. Room #3 served as a combination saloon and card room, where Josephine's husband, Anacleto, presided over a long mahogany bar, serving drinks to weary travelers, farmers, ranchers and miners.

In 1962, the property was purchased by Margaret Dienelt, who renamed it the Gunn House Hotel. She added the beautifully landscaped garden patio and swimming pool. In 2002, innkeepers Mike and Shirley Sarno bought it and undertook an impressive restoration of the historic structure. The original adobe, which makes up the central core of the house, remains intact, with newer additions on both sides.

GHOSTS

An old building like the Gunn House is likely to harbor a few spirits from the past, and innkeeper Shirley Sarno has had her share of unusual encounters. She says that every once in a while, objects will jump off the shelves or unexpectedly disappear. Employees have noticed unusual creaks and squeaks in the old wooden floors, and fleeting, dark shadows have been seen on the stairs. Rooms in the old original section of the inn seem to have more ghostly activity.

A housekeeper, who has worked at the hotel for over forty years, has a repertoire of interesting stories about her experiences. One of her favorites involved a couple who'd spent the night in Room #11. They enjoyed a restful night's sleep, but when they awoke in the morning, they were surprised to see every one of the pictures and mirrors in the room were hanging on the wall cockeyed. Since there were a total of thirteen that were askew, and they had been straight the evening before, the couple wondered if invisible hands had been at work. They had not heard any unusual noises during the night, and there had not been any earthquakes, so what disturbed the wall décor?

One very skeptical guest, who stayed in Room #10, was disturbed by the bed shaking beneath him. This lasted about fifteen minutes, and there was no reason for this activity. One night, a couple in Room #9 was awakened when they felt that someone was trying to join them in bed. When the husband got up to investigate and opened the room's door, he felt a presence actually shove him out into the hall, slamming the door behind him. Since his wife was still in bed when this happened, the aggravated guest wondered if there really was a third presence in their room.

The original building has been incorporated into the structure seen today. *Wendy Williams.*

The longtime housekeeper reported that when she and another employee were working in the parlor, they were suddenly startled by a tall woman, dressed in gray, who emerged from the fireplace. She appeared to be dragging something made of a darker gray material, and she walked through the parlor, passing directly through its solid wooden doors.

A woman who stayed in Room #12 claimed that she opened the closet door and was terrified to see a "hideous face" peering back at her. Some guests have been awakened to see the full body apparition of a man standing at the foot of their bed. Paranormal experts say that some of this ghostly activity may date back to the thirty years that the Gunn House was operated as a hospital.

When paranormal investigator Wendy Williams visited the hotel, she obtained high EMF readings in Room #3. She stayed in one of the upstairs rooms and remarked, "I felt like someone was watching me in the upstairs hallway, but there was never anyone around." The area behind the hotel was once the play yard for the five Gunn children. They weren't allowed in the front yard, which faced busy Washington Street and was always crowded with wagons, horses, mules and foot traffic.

The Gunn House has eighteen guest rooms, beautifully decorated with period furnishings and antiques. Front rooms open on the shady balcony, where old rocking chairs invite you to sit and relax. This is a great spot that overlooks the main thoroughfare, bustling with activity, just as it did more than 160 years ago.

SONORA INN

The Spanish façade of the Sonora Inn/Days Inn catches your eye when you come into town. It sits on land that once bordered the old Central Plaza, which was lined with canvas tents, flimsy board shacks and lean-tos, hastily thrown up after gold was discovered. Throngs of miners once stomped down the wooden plank walkways in front of the early saloons, gambling houses and shops. Sonora was the most ethnically diverse settlement in the Gold Country, and it was the only town with a significant number of women.

Most of the temporary structures around the Plaza went up in flames in the Great Sonora Fire of 1852. In 1854, Mary Bailey built a boardinghouse near the Plaza. She was the first woman in the Mother Lode country to take advantage of a new law that allowed married women to carry on business in their own names. Mary's boardinghouse was an immediate success, and she operated it for several years before deciding to sell. When she turned the boardinghouse over to its new owner, it became the American Hotel. After a few years, it was again sold to become the Sonora Hotel and later the Stage Hotel.

In 1896, Captain William Nevills purchased the building and began construction of a palatial establishment, which he dubbed the Hotel Victoria. The wealthy Nevills was a prominent citizen and owner of the rich Rawhide Mine in nearby Jamestown. He often traveled about the Gold Country on business and was easily spotted in his elegant carriage, with its beautiful team of horses that was guided by a liveried driver.

Nevills expected to be treated with fawning respect and would hold a grudge if he didn't get it. Once on a trip to Sonora, he was unable to rent a room at the City Hotel. Ignoring the fact that the place was full, he became enraged. Waving his fists and stomping about the lobby, Nevills shouted, "I'll build a hotel across the street and run you right out of business!" Biding his time, when the Stage Hotel went on the market, Nevills snatched it up and transformed it into the elegant Hotel Victoria, his weapon of revenge.

The palatial Hotel Victoria was built by wealthy William Nevills in 1896 on a site adjacent to Sonora's old town plaza. *Courtesy of Tuolumne County Historical Society.*

The Victoria's fancy façade was covered with stucco and became the Mission-style Sonora Inn when this type of design swept California. *Wendy Williams.*

Built of slate and rock from the surrounding hills, the elegant hotel had all the modern conveniences, including electric lights, a bathroom on each floor and a large bar glittering with mirrors and luxurious velvet banquettes. Guests were greeted in a spacious lobby, paneled with gleaming mahogany and lovely redwood. Fine crystal chandeliers illuminated the collection of expensive artwork and beautiful paintings. There was a comfortable lounge where ladies were welcome to sit and chat or have a cup of tea. There were two plush dining rooms, where guests feasted on a variety of steaks and lobster and drank the best wines from the hotel's wine cellar. They were serenaded by classical musicians, and the orchestra played as guests took a spin around the large ballroom. The state-of-the-art elevator whisked guests from the lobby upstairs to their elegantly furnished rooms.

One end of the hotel was dominated by a round tower with a weathervane, and an elaborate façade ran along the front of the building. There were long balconies on the second and third floors where guests could watch passengers board the Wells Fargo stage headed for Yosemite. The Hotel Victoria became an important fixture in the Sonora social scene, and old newspaper clippings are full of stories of many grand events that were held here.

A terrible fire in 1931 severely damaged the hotel, which was eventually repaired, but it never regained its earlier luxury. When the Spanish California craze swept the area, its fancy Victorian façade was covered with stucco and hidden away behind Mission-style arched colonnades. A red tile roof capped the transformation and fall from grand Victorian hotel to a California motel.

GHOSTS

This old hotel has an impish ghost, a little girl who likes the building's upstairs halls. A small shadowy figure has been seen bouncing a ball down the long third-floor hallway and around Room #309. Guests are surprised when they fling open their doors, only to discover no one is there, and they often complain about the noise.

When a guest tries to use the old elevator, it is usually uncooperative, but it often runs up and down between floors at night when it has no passengers. Is a mysterious little finger pushing the buttons and giggling merrily as the old car rumbles noisily between floors, disturbing and frightening guests?

Chapter 15

JAMESTOWN

The hillsides around Jamestown were once alight with prospectors' campfires as the easy findings of gold drew many to this part of the Mother Lode. In 1848, Benjamin Wood found gold in a small creek, and a little settlement called "Woods Crossing" developed. When a gold nugget weighing 195 pounds was found at nearby Carson Hill, the rush really gained momentum.

The lure of gold drew flamboyant Colonel George James, who set up his trading business in a huge tent. Although he was in a rugged environment, the colonel refused to give up his lavish lifestyle, and his tent was stacked with oysters, wines and tins of crackers and sardines. The colonel sold groceries, sundries, picks, shovels, gold pans and mining equipment and did very well, but he wasn't satisfied with honest wealth. The colonel wanted more, and he began to hatch clever schemes to separate the miners from their gold dust.

As Colonel James's influence among the prospectors grew, the bustling camp changed its name in his honor, dubbing the place "Jamestown," and they even named him its first *alcalde*. In the Mexican legal system, an *alcalde* is a combination mayor, judge, city clerk and legal advisor, so this civic duty gave Woods much greater power.

When the easy findings of gold near the creek declined, Jamestown was moved east about a mile and closer to Table Mountain. Using his official capacity to his advantage, the colonel became a gold speculator, and one evening, after plying several miners with a great deal of champagne, he persuaded them to turn over their hard-earned gold to invest in his scheme.

Imagine these prospectors waking the next morning to massive headaches and the fact that the illustrious colonel had disappeared, taking their gold dust with him. The bilked investors tried to track down the scoundrel, but despite vigorous searches, they were unsuccessful. Disappointed and angry about their losses, they voted to immediately change the name of their town to "American Camp." Unfortunately, everyone was used to the old name, and the new moniker of American Camp did not catch on. So when the community was awarded a post office in 1853, the official name reverted back to Jamestown or "Jimtown," as many preferred.

Jamestown became a center of mining, transportation and trade activity, and it grew rapidly. It was home to many businesses, including a bank, drugstores, doctors' offices, livery stables, restaurants, hotels, saloons and butcher shops. The Jamestown Methodist Church, built in 1852, did dual duty as a house of worship on Sundays and a school for the town's youngsters during the week.

When the rich placer deposits were exhausted, newly discovered quartz gold veins led to underground hardrock mining. By the late 1880s, pneumatic drills had been developed, making it much easier to place dynamite for blasting. Better techniques for extracting gold from rock were successful, and Jamestown boomed, the center of the area's quartz mining. The App Mine on Quartz Mountain, which operated until 1909, produced $6.5 million, while the Rawhide, considered one of the greatest mines in the world, also produced over $6 million worth of gold.

A new steam railroad, the Sierra Railway built in 1897, hauled ore from this isolated mountain community to the valley mills for processing. Its lines were extended into the forests for lumbering and to carry the wood down to the valley towns. From there, it was shipped all over California for building.

In 1896, a devastating fire wiped out much of Jamestown and killed several people. The town was rebuilt, and the economy boomed during the construction of the O'Shaughnessy Dam and the Hetch Hetchy Water Project to provide water to the Bay Area. This mammoth undertaking consumed twenty-five years, and it brought work crews, engineers and railroaders into Jamestown. They spent money for rooms and in the town's shops, saloons and restaurants.

When the government shut down gold mining in 1942, Jamestown's citizens developed new enterprises that included gambling halls and a booming red-light district. California's attorney general put a damper on these thriving businesses in 1952, so farsighted citizens turned their attention

Main Street of Jamestown when it became an important railroad center, shipping lumber and supplies for the Hetch Hetchy Water Project. *Courtesy of Tuolumne County Historical Society.*

to the movies. Hard work and ingenuity brought the movie companies to town with their glamorous stars and demanding producers. The Sierra Railroad's Locomotive #3 became a movie star and appeared in over two hundred films, pulling its rail cars through passes, often waylaid by bandits. The engine whistled and chugged its way through *Butch Cassidy and the Sundance Kid, High Noon, Bad Day at Black Rock, Petticoat Junction* and many more thrillers and TV programs.

JAMESTOWN TODAY

Although several of Jamestown's original structures were destroyed by fire, it retains the flavor of a picturesque, Old West community. Many of its elderly, balconied buildings lining Main Street were once stores that supplied citizens with merchandise and supplies. Now they are occupied by gift and souvenir shops, antique emporiums and restaurants. A few old stone relics hide their history behind coats of stucco, but the thickness of the walls around the windows and doors reveals their true age.

The town's worn boardwalks, nineteenth-century wooden balconies and false-fronted stores continue to attract movie companies and TV crews.

Take a close look, and you'll recognize Main Street, where Gary Cooper stood alone to meet the enemy, seeking revenge at *High Noon*. Clint Eastwood in *Pale Rider* knew these dusty streets and might have stopped in the saloon for a cool one.

NATIONAL HOTEL

This hotel on Main Street is one of the state's oldest, and it has been in continuous operation since its debut in 1859. The first owners, Heinrich and Hannah Neilson, combined two of the oldest buildings in Jamestown into a saloon, restaurant and hotel. The wooden building escaped the fire of 1896, but it was severely damaged by flames in 1901, when several blocks of the town were completely destroyed. In 1927, another fire burned down an adjacent building and damaged the National so severely that it had to be completely rebuilt.

During Prohibition, the hotel's saloon was raided several times, and its secret stores of illegal booze were seized. The January 5, 1927 issue of the *Union Democrat* reported that government agents had again pounced on the National, confiscating several fifty-gallon and one-hundred-gallon barrels of wine, plus numerous kegs of brandy and whiskey. Owner Joe Graziano was fined $500, but it didn't deter him from continuing his lucrative business. Legalized prostitution was another sideline activity, and this enterprise thrived until the late 1930s. Gambling was legal, and there were plenty of slot machines at the hotel until 1949. The hotel had some permanent boarders, who paid $60 a month for a room and the luxury of inside plumbing, sharing a toilet, sink and bathtub.

In 1974, the National Hotel was sold to Steve and Michel Willey, who've been operating it for over thirty-two years. They renovated the old building themselves and restored the hotel to its original condition, with some modern additions. The plumbing and electrical systems were updated and private baths added. The hotel's restaurant, which hadn't served a meal since 1946, was redone, as well as two smaller dining rooms. Much of the dining room's original wood wainscoting was preserved, and the old front balcony was restored, following the 1850s design. The saloon, with its metal ceiling, antique back bar and 1881 cash register, is an authentic gold rush survivor.

Steve Willey says he was unaware of the hotel's paranormal activity, but once he moved in, things began to happen. Employees, guests and locals told him about Flo, a hotel resident who has never left. Flo arrived at the

Jamestown train station in the 1890s and rented a room at the National Hotel. She was a friendly young woman who shared her story of unexpected romance with other guests. Flo was traveling by train from the East to visit relatives in San Francisco. She met a fellow passenger named Henry, a handsome young lawyer, and it was love at first sight. During their journey, Henry proposed marriage, and Flo quickly accepted. They planned to meet again in Jamestown in six weeks, after Flo visited her relatives, and Henry started his new job.

A few days before Christmas, the young couple was joyfully reunited and went to the National Hotel. Flo hired a dressmaker to start sewing her wedding gown, and on Christmas morning, Henry presented her with a beautiful diamond ring. The next day, Flo was waiting in the hotel restaurant to share breakfast with Henry when there was a sudden gunshot. Everyone ran toward the commotion, and Flo was horrified to find Henry lying in a pool of blood at the bottom of the staircase, near the open front door. Cradling him in her arms, Flo begged Henry to live, but love couldn't conquer a fatal gunshot, and he drew his last breath, whispering his love.

The National Hotel has been in continuous operation since it opened in 1859. *Wendy Williams.*

No one knows how this terrible tragedy happened, and no one was ever arrested for the fatal shooting. It's believed that a drunken man stumbled in the front door of the hotel and, waving his gun about, accidentally discharged the pistol, hitting Henry in the chest as he was coming down the stairs.

Flo was inconsolable. Instead of planning a wedding, she was faced with a funeral. She sat for days in her room, staring out the window, ignoring the kindly hotel staff. They tried to coax her to have a comforting cup of tea or a bowl of soup, but she tearfully refused. Uncontrollable sobs and terrible cries came from Flo's lonely front room, day and night. Then on New Year's Eve, there were no more sobs, only silence. The housekeeper peeked in and saw Flo, in her beautiful wedding gown, sitting by the window. When she approached the young woman, the housekeeper was horrified to see that she was not breathing. The doctor was summoned, but it was too late. The cause of her death was listed as heart failure. However, those who are wise in matters of love know that Flo really died of a broken heart.

GHOSTS

Flo has made the National Hotel her permanent home, and although tragedy visited her here, she is usually a cheerful presence as she roams the halls. She occasionally tosses pans and pots about in the kitchen and sets the spoons and ladles swinging wildly on their hooks. She seems to be a playful spirit, but occasionally sobs will be heard in the upper halls, usually at night. Members of the hotel staff have seen a wispy shadow coming down the stairs in the morning, and it often floats right through the dining room walls.

Willey says that his guests and employees have had many encounters with Flo. Housekeepers have reported placing a stack of clean towels on one side of a bed, then after turning their backs for a minute, they find the towels mysteriously moved to the opposite side of the bed. Window shades are opened after they were closed by housekeeping, and the dining room staff has seen a woman in a long gown, waiting to enter, but then she mysteriously disappears.

Steve Willey only had one encounter with Flo. It happened one afternoon when he was standing on the front porch of his home, directly behind the hotel. There was no breeze that day, but suddenly one of the large wind chimes hanging on the eaves began ringing loudly. None of the other smaller, lighter wind chimes moved, but the sound from the large chime grew in intensity. Willey walked up to it, and the ringing stopped suddenly. When he turned to go into the house, several of the wind chimes again began ringing and moving about as if they were being shaken by invisible hands. As before, there was no breeze. On a whim, Willey commanded, "Flo, stop it!" Immediately, the movement and sounds of the wind chimes stopped.

Many hotel guests have recorded their observations in a journal kept in each room. The hotel's lights often flicker or go off completely, and doors slam unexpectedly. Guests have found their clothes tossed about and their suitcases dumped on the floor. Other times, a suitcase has been carefully unpacked, and the clothing arranged neatly in the closet. Flo seems to favor the front rooms on the second floor, and some guests have sensed an unseen presence in this hall. Others have felt sudden, icy blasts of air in a cozy, warm room.

JAMESTOWN HOTEL

The Jamestown Hotel, built in 1858, was a miners' boardinghouse until it was destroyed by the huge fire of 1896. When rebuilt, it became a bordello, operating until 1919, when it was sold and converted into a hotel. In 1938, Dr. D.L. Farrell purchased the wooden frame building, covered the outer walls with brick and transformed the old hotel into the Mother Lode Hospital.

One spring, a beautiful, young redheaded woman got off the train in Jamestown and walked up Main Street to the hospital. Her name was Mary Rose Sullivan, and after consultation, Dr. Farrell admitted her to Room #7. The quiet young woman usually remained in her room, spending most of her days gazing out the window at the surrounding hills. It was soon evident that she was pregnant and alone, but she confided in no one. When labor began, dire complications developed, and despite Dr. Farrell's efforts, both Mary Rose and her baby died. They were buried in the small cemetery overlooking Jamestown.

Several weeks after these tragic deaths, the hospital's night nurse was startled when she heard soft moans coming from Room #7. Since there were no patients in there, she hurried to investigate. When she opened the door, it was quite dark, but there was a soft glow of light around the bed. Then the frightened nurse saw a luminous image and screamed in horror as the gruesome specter of a man wrapped in chains slowly materialized. She rushed from the room, slammed the door and anxiously waited for morning.

The Jamestown Hotel, built in 1858, was a miners' boardinghouse and saloon. It was destroyed in the 1896 fire and then rebuilt. *Courtesy of Tuolumne County Historical Society.*

When the nurse told Dr. Farrell about her experience, he sighed and said that he must share Mary Rose's story. The physician said Mary Rose had told him about a young man, named Frank Sullivan, who'd come to Jamestown in the 1850s and had made a lucky gold strike. He'd returned to his native Ireland but often told his young granddaughter, Mary Rose, about his adventures in California.

When she grew older, Mary Rose fell in love with a British soldier, and the couple planned to marry. However, the soldier's family opposed their marriage plans and arranged to have their young soldier son sent off to India, far from Mary Rose. Unfortunately, he was captured during an uprising, thrown into chains and kept imprisoned in a dungeon there. He was tortured and eventually died in captivity.

When Mary Rose learned of her lover's death, she was grief-stricken and fled from Ireland, making her way to California and on to Jamestown. She had told no one in Ireland that she was expecting the soldier's baby. She implored the doctor to keep her secret. He agreed to delivery her baby and promised to help her start a new life in Jamestown. Instead, both died in Room #7.

History is vague about the intervening years, but in the 1950s, the old hospital closed. A few years later, it was reopened as a boardinghouse. During the 1970s, it changed hands, underwent extensive renovations and was transformed into an eleven-room hotel. Now, once again, the Jamestown Hotel has new owners. While remodeling, they discovered a large dumbwaiter that dates back to the hospital days. It was used to move supplies and—it's rumored—also carry bodies to the basement morgue.

GHOSTS

Guests report hearing soft moans and sighs coming from Room #7, and recently one woman said she had been kept awake much of the night by occasional screams. She seemed quite frightened by her experiences. Guests request this room but often ask to be moved because they become so uneasy that they can't sleep.

The Jamestown Hotel once served this community as the Mother Lode Hospital. *Wendy Williams.*

Sometimes, guests who peeked into #7 said they saw a strange, glowing light when there was no moon. Others have described this phenomenon as similar to a faint, eerie shadow. Once in a while, a wispy image has been seen in the hall near #7. Guests record their experiences in journals that are in each room, and several noted cold spots and chill drafts upstairs. Others heard soft footsteps in the night. A few even said there were strange noises that sounded like the rattling of chains.

Chapter 16

GROVELAND

A short jaunt on State Route 120, off Highway 49, takes you up a steep, corkscrew climb through brushy hillsides, dotted with scattered oaks to the quiet village of Big Oak Flat. Originally called Savage's Diggings, gold was discovered here by James Savage, a friend of the Indians, who operated several trading posts. He hired many loyal Indians to work the streams for gold. When the rich placer deposits of Savage's Diggings became overrun with eager gold seekers, Savage moved on, and in 1851, he was the first white man to discover the wonders of Yosemite.

Over $28 million in gold was unearthed around Big Oak Flat, which quickly grew into a lively camp. A huge oak tree, over thirteen feet thick, stood near the middle of town until 1869 when it, too, became a victim of gold fever. Prospectors undermined its roots, ferreting out gold nuggets concealed in its gnarled underpinnings, and the once handsome giant eventually died, a victim of greed. A monument marks the place where this huge oak, acclaimed as the largest in California, once stood.

In the early days, a couple men, said to be Mexican, stole some gold dust, and others rushed to deliver swift justice. A fine oak was selected, and the pair was quickly strung up. The camp immediately became known as "Garotte," the Spanish word for a punishment involving strangling. When history repeated itself about two miles south, another fine oak hosted the second necktie party. This camp became "Second Garotte," making the other "First Garotte."

Both mining camps earned their grim names because their citizens tended to act first and debate later. Once a suspect was captured in First Garotte, court would be convened over the bar, and it didn't take long to reach a verdict. Hanging became a regular spur-of-the-moment event, and the sound of frontier justice was a tap dance of boot heels and the jingling of spurs as the culprit dangled from the oak tree.

Years after the camp's vigilante days had passed, the hanging tree, a large oak, still stood in an alley behind the Hotel Charlotte. It eventually became an obstruction for the four-wheeled vehicles that were replacing horses and pack trains, and it was cut down. The large stump was sawed flat so it was even with the alley's firmly packed ground, and lifelong residents of Groveland remember running over this hard, wooden circle in the alley as children. Eventually, the stump splintered and was dug up, and the hole was filled with earth, leaving only the gnarled roots below.

Two miles to the southeast, the stark remnant of Second Garotte's hanging tree looms by the side of the road, its bare branches like skeletal fingers thrust toward the sky. There's no tally sheet or record of the number of unfortunates who were hoisted into the hereafter at this dismal spot, but the tree's massive trunk bears a marker testifying to its notorious past. Nearby is a weathered frame house that's over one hundred years old and was built by two miners, who spent their lives here. When writer Bret Harte lived in Second Garotte, this pair inspired his story *Tennessee's Partner*.

After 1870, the placer deposits were exhausted, and the local population dwindled to around one hundred. They toughed it out with cattle ranching and, in 1875, concerned about appearances, changed the name of their hamlet to "Groveland." They benefited when gold prices rose in the late 1890s. Deep mining shafts were sunk to tap the rich gold quartz deposits, and the stamp mills again thundered, crushing rock day and night. When the price of gold fell, Groveland declined again.

In 1914, Groveland became construction headquarters for the Hetch Hetchy Water Project, designed to meet the growing need for water in San Francisco and the Bay area. An ambitious plan was developed to dam the Tuolumne River that meandered through Hetch Hetchy, a wide, glacial valley as grand as Yosemite. Before the dam could be built, the Hetch Hetchy Railroad was constructed, extending the Sierra Railroad from Jamestown to the future dam site. It would haul cement, materials and workers to build the O'Shaughnessy Dam.

From 1915 through 1925, construction crews, railroad men and their families poured into Groveland. There was plenty of work building the new dam and bridges and completing the Yosemite Valley Railroad from Merced. This would be the first train bringing tourists in comfortable passenger cars to see the wonders of Yosemite Valley.

The Hotel Charlotte was the realization of the dream of hardworking Charlotte DeFerrari.
Courtesy of California State Library History Room.

GROVELAND TODAY

Groveland's Main Street is lined with old false-front and turn-of-the-century structures that house interesting shops and colorful stores. They welcome travelers, willing to stray a few miles from Highway 49 to enjoy a touch of the past. There are many reminders of Groveland's boom days, including two old hotels, which have some permanent guests from another era.

The Iron Door Saloon, which claims to be the oldest establishment serving liquor in California, started in the Granite Store, built in 1852. The bar was a wooden plank over flour barrels in a corner of the mercantile, where liquor was served to thirsty prospectors. The business was sold to Jim Tannahill, the town's postmaster, in the 1860s, and it served as a store and the post office for twenty-five years. In 1896, Giacomo DeFerrari bought it, turning it into a full-fledged saloon, which he called Jake's Place.

To protect the building from fire, iron doors and shutters, manufactured in England, were installed. They had sailed around Cape Horn, been hauled inland by mule-drawn wagons, crossed the Tuolumne River by ferry and finally arrived in Groveland. In 1937, the historic establishment's name was changed to the Iron Door Saloon, and with its old back bar and stray bullet holes, it's a lively remnant of the Mother Lode's wildest days.

HOTEL CHARLOTTE

In 1897, when she was sixteen, Charlotte DeFerrari came to California with her mother and two brothers from Genoa, Italy. Their father, Luigi, and his brothers had immigrated during the early days of the gold rush. While working the family mining claim near Groveland, a tunnel had suddenly caved in, killing him and injuring his brother. Learning of the disaster, Charlotte's mother decided to bring her family to America to be near her husband's relatives in Groveland.

Young Charlotte became the family's sole breadwinner, cooking for work crews and cowboys. She eventually became a cook at a local ranch, where her delicious Italian meals brought droves of hungry men to her long board table. Charlotte worked hard, saved her money and dreamed of one day owning her own restaurant.

Her uncle, Giacomo DeFerrari, had good luck mining and acquired enough gold to invest in real estate. He bought the Tannahill Store and expanded the liquor business into his saloon, Jake's Place. He offered her space in his building, where Charlotte opened her first small restaurant. Charlotte did well, and the news of the planned Hetch Hetchy Reservoir spurred her to build a boardinghouse on the site of an old Main Street livery stable. The young businesswoman knew that the hundreds of workers who would swell Groveland's population would need a place to sleep and eat. When the Hotel Charlotte opened its doors, its rooms were quickly filled, and it became a home away from home for men involved with the dam project. Managers from San Francisco stayed on for months, overseeing the work, and paying their bills regularly. Charlotte decided that this was the time to expand, and in 1921, she purchased the Gem Saloon next door. She remodeled the place, and it became another successful restaurant.

Charlotte DeFerrari was respected for her honesty and hard work and became an important voice in Groveland. Always involved in civic activities, she offered a helping hand to others and enjoyed meeting tourists visiting Yosemite. There were rumors of a romance with a San Francisco gentleman who stayed in Room #6, but Charlotte's first love was her hotel and the little mountain town. She continued to operate the Hotel Charlotte until sometime in the 1940s, when she finally decided to sell.

Charlotte died in November 1970 and was mourned by the entire community. She was buried in nearby Big Oak Flat, but many believe she's still around, keeping an eye on her hotel.

GHOSTS

This attractive old hotel, with its comfortable rooms, welcomes travelers and tempts them to stay a while. The front balcony is an ideal spot to relax and watch passersby on Main Street, just as visitors did a century ago. Guests in Room #6 often say that they feel pampered and especially well cared for. The hotel owner usually gives that room to single men because Charlotte checks to see that they are comfortable. Maybe she tucks them in on chilly nights.

There are stories that an image of Charlotte is occasionally seen in an antique mirror that hangs in Room #6, and some guests have even tried to photograph this mysterious lady. Hotel owners Doug and Jenn Edwards welcome guests, and they may be joined now and then by the industrious Charlotte. She's reluctant to say good-bye to her hotel and restaurant, the true passions of her life.

GROVELAND HOTEL

This old hotel has had many past lives and has undergone several reincarnations since it was an adobe trading post back in 1849. It had its rowdy days as a saloon and gambling hall, and as a hotel during the gold rush, it was described by travelers as "the best house on the hill." In 1914, it was purchased by the county's most successful cattleman, Timothy Carlton. He leased the hotel to Walter Pechart, known as "Peach," who quickly converted it into a sporting house. With the girls, gambling and slot machines, the old hotel was hopping twenty-four hours a day. Both the town and the hotel thrived as a result of the Hetch Hetchy project that brought hundreds of workers to town.

When the state clamped down on gambling and vice, the Groveland Hotel was sold and became a staid office building. It housed lawyers and the Forest Service headquarters and even welcomed thrifty travelers as a stop on the Greyhound Bus line. When it was no longer needed, the old building sat empty for years, collecting rainwater, mice and bugs. A family of feral cats

The Groveland Hotel can trace its history back to 1849 and is home to Lyle, an old dynamiter who's made this his permanent home. *Courtesy of Tuolumne County Historical Society.*

made their home in one of its original adobe walls, and the hotel became a forlorn derelict on Main Street.

In 1990, with foreclosure and complete disintegration looming, the old relic was rescued by its present owners, Peggy and Grover Mosley. Two years and a lot of money went into restoring the hotel to its once grand nineteenth-century style. As a concession to modern needs, guest bathrooms were added and WiFi capabilities increased. It is one of the few old buildings in the Sierra Nevada that was constructed in the Monterey Colonial architectural style.

GHOSTS

A stay in Room #15 will quickly convince you that stories about messy bachelors aren't always true. The ghost named Lyle, who calls this room home, is very neat and tidy and frequently "straightens up." Longtime Groveland resident Ernie Greenbeck recalled Lyle as a bachelor, who arrived after the boom days of the gold rush. He was a dynamite expert, who had plenty of work handling the stuff and blasting glory holes for others. He took a room at the Groveland Hotel, a boardinghouse in those days, staying at least six years. Lyle minded his own business, and when he wasn't blasting, he prospected in the area's creeks.

In 1927, Lyle failed to appear at the dinner table for several evenings, and his fellow boarders became concerned because it wasn't like Lyle to miss a meal. When they checked his room, they found the old miner lying stretched out on his bed, as dead as yesterday. Lyle was taken away to a new home in the cemetery, and his neatly folded clothes were removed from the dresser. Under the bed, the hotel owner was horrified to find a box of dynamite, the tool of Lyle's trade. His room, #15, was spiffed up, but the staff had little to do because he'd been an ideal boarder, neat and fastidious, keeping his possessions orderly and his room tidy.

Although Lyle left his earthly home back in 1927, the hotel's current owner, Peggy Mosley, believes this neat boarder has stayed on. His dresser remains in this room, and he doesn't like women's cosmetics sitting on it. Peggy Mosley says, "He often removes them," adding that some guests even asked if these items should be kept off the dresser since they'd been moved so many times. Makeup is usually found on the bathroom sink. One lady saw her cosmetics take a sudden dive to the floor, while another swears that she saw them being moved as she watched.

Lyle doesn't care for bright lights, and they are often dimmed or even turned out while a guest in #15 is reading. One evening while Peggy was hosting a dinner party, the dining room lights started fluctuating from bright to dim. This suddenly stopped, and everyone in the room felt a whoosh of cold air rush past. Peggy recalled, "We all gasped, and it really was a hair-raising experience!"

Another evening, the chef placed several loaves of bread into the oven to bake but forgot to set the oven timer. Peggy was working in the kitchen and said, "We were all busy, but everyone was startled when the oven doors suddenly flew open—just when the bread had been baked perfectly!" Was Lyle keeping an eye on it? The old dynamiter spends a lot of time in the kitchen and dining room, where most of the staff has had at least one encounter with him.

Now and then, a shadowy figure is seen in the hall or one of the bedrooms, as if someone is making the rounds and checking to see that all is well. Occasionally, Lyle is gone for a few weeks, and there's speculation that he's visiting a home he left long ago or catching up on lost memories with a mysterious lady friend. Some folks believe that Lyle might be just up the street, visiting Charlotte, the proprietor of her namesake hotel. Wherever Lyle goes on his sojourns, he always returns to his home at the Groveland Hotel.

Chapter 17

COULTERVILLE

Coulterville is a small shadow of its former self, a once bustling mining camp. This remnant of the gold rush is rustic and a bit plain, with few glimmers of its vibrant and volatile past. There has been little restoration, and the entire town has been designated a State Historic Landmark. Main Street, on the National Register of Historic Places, looks tired and worn, with its weathered, old buildings and sun-baked adobe walls.

The camp was started in 1850 by George Coulter, a merchant who set up a large, blue canvas tent store on the banks of a seasonal stream. The miners, drawn by the area's rich, gold-bearing quartz ledges, were predominantly Mexicans, so George stuck an American flag above his store, and the camp was called "Bandereta" or "Little Flag." When George Maxwell, another merchant, showed up, he suggested the town needed a better name and proposed "Maxwellville." Straws were drawn, and Coulter won the contest. The camp became "Coulterville," and Maxwell's name was given to the nearby creek.

Because Coulterville was separated from other Mother Lode settlements by miles of rugged terrain, it quickly became prosperous, providing supplies to more than two thousand miners. It blossomed from a tent city into an adobe and brick boomtown. Single-story adobe buildings, stores, saloons, rooming houses and hotels were built by immigrants flooding in from Italy, France, Great Britain, Canada and even Persia. Its Chinatown, with over 1,500 people, was one of the largest in the Gold Country. Coulterville soon had a population of 5,000, with ten hotels, twenty-five saloons and dozens of stores and shops. Nelson Cody, brother of Buffalo Bill Cody, was the Wells Fargo agent in 1870 and also served as the town's postmaster.

By 1859, when the rich placer deposits began to decline, the prospectors scrabbled in the dirt, cursed the labor and hoped to find a few more glints of gold. Hardrock quartz mining began in earnest, and men gave up their picks, pans and independence and went to work for the company mines. Pack trains of noisy burros, loaded with supplies, crowded Main Street, while stages, crammed with passengers and chests of gold bullion, clattered out of town, headed for San Francisco. Over the next fifty years, the Mary Harrison Mine and others produced millions of dollars in gold, contributing to the town's continuing prosperity.

On the Fourth of July in 1859, the first disastrous fire wiped out the business district, leaving only smoldering embers, bare rock walls and gutted buildings. Undaunted, the citizens rebuilt on a grander scale, installing fine chandeliers, expensive mirrors and hand-carved walnut bars in the saloons and hotels. In 1862, a major flood wreaked havoc, and all buildings that were located along Maxwell Creek were destroyed or heavily damaged.

During the 1860s, interest in the newly discovered Yosemite Valley spurred the first tourist travel through Coulterville. Since the valley could only be

During the 1870s, stages departed from the Jeffery, taking tourists to see the wonders of Yosemite. *Courtesy of California State Library History Room.*

reached by a hazardous journey over steep, precipitous trails on foot, mule or horseback, the need for a safe stage route was obvious. In 1871, the town's businessmen organized the Coulterville and Yosemite Turnpike Company to build a road into the Yosemite Valley.

It took three years to complete this road, and the company had to overcome fierce competition and a constant lack of money. Its drive and determination succeeded, and the first stage thundered triumphantly into Yosemite Valley in June 1874. More followed, carrying Horace Greeley, Ralph Waldo Emerson and Thomas Edison, who spread the word about the beauty of this valley. Just as Coulterville had monopolized the mining supply business, it now controlled the Yosemite tourist trade.

In July 1879, another fire wiped out much of the town, but again the citizens rebuilt. The Merced Gold Mining Company constructed the county's first narrow-gauge railroad from the Mary Harrison Mine to the stamp mill. The company bought an eight-ton steam locomotive, which was shipped around South America's Cape Horn to Stockton. Then it was hauled up steep grades by a giant team of thirty-six mules, pulling a sturdy logging wagon that carried the engine. Dubbed "Whistling Billy," this engine was put to work pulling fifteen ore cars that weighed five tons each. It steamed around the curves and switchbacks of the "Crookedest Railroad in the World."

In July 1899, a third major fire destroyed much of Coulterville, and this time, many folks decided it was time to move on. The population dwindled even more when many young men, anticipating the end of the gold mining industry, left to work on the reconstruction of San Francisco after the 1906 earthquake and fire. In 1913, when a portion of the Coulterville Road into Yosemite became a public highway, the first autos were welcomed into town by a population that had dropped to six hundred. Ten years later, there were only three hundred folks calling Coulterville home.

Today, an influx of urban refugees has joined the remaining descendants of the town's first miners, merchants and settlers. Coulterville and the surrounding area now boast a population of around two thousand people.

HOTEL JEFFERY

This building was known as the "Adobe" when George Jeffery bought it in 1851. It housed a store with a fandango hall on the second floor, and it had been built in the 1840s by early Mexican settlers. Its sturdy walls were made of adobe and rock and were about three feet thick. Jeffery converted it to a three-story hotel, offering the latest in comfort to travelers and weary miners. Downstairs, there was a lobby, and thirsty guests could belly up to the bar in its rip-roaring Magnolia Saloon.

The Hotel Jeffery was gutted by fire in July 1859, leaving only its thick adobe walls. When rebuilt, these original walls were incorporated into the new building. Twenty years later, in July 1879, there was another fire, but the hotel escaped this time. After twenty years, a third devastating fire in July 1899 burned the hotel to the ground. Never ones to give up, the Jeffery family again rebuilt, and today's hotel welcomes guests just as it has over the last one hundred years.

The Hotel Jeffery is one of California's oldest and has been owned and operated for generations by the same family. A review of old Coulterville business directories and town records show that year after year, a Jeffery descendant has remained in control of the hotel. Sons were born, grew up and took over, and when daughters married, they and their husbands assumed its responsibility. As late as 1960, the Jeffery Hotel was operated by Ed Sackett, who married Violet Thompson, the granddaughter of the original owner, George Jeffery.

When she was a young girl, Violet's parents, John Thompson and Sarah Jeffery Thompson, told stories about her grandfather and how hard he worked to make his hotel successful. Determined to hold his own against the nine hotels that were quickly built to accommodate the town's burgeoning population, George Jeffery turned his old adobe store–fandango hall into a gracious hostelry, welcoming travelers, mining engineers, merchants and businessmen.

For years, Ed and Violet Sackett operated the hotel, which was the social center of Coulterville during the 1960s. There were plenty of meetings and parties, and folks dropped by to chat or have a drink at the Magnolia. A door had been made through the hotel wall directly into the saloon, a convenience for guests who wanted to quench their thirst. Ed oversaw all the activities in the hotel, the Magnolia Saloon and the restaurant.

When Violet died, Sackett stayed on for many more years, taking care of the place that had become his home. Ed Sackett died around 1975, and since he had no children to inherit the hotel, it was boarded up and sat vacant. During the 1980s, a group of investors bought the old structure and began renovations. It's now in the hands of owners Forrest Monk and Sara Zahn.

The Jeffery is one of California's oldest hotels. Built in the 1840s, it has been operated by generations of the same family. *Wendy Williams.*

GHOSTS

As early as the 1980s, an older man, who resembled photos of Ed Sackett, was seen in the restaurant and around the hotel. No one knew who he was, and he'd be in sight one minute and vanish the next. When renovations were finished, this same man was often seen sitting quietly in a corner of the dining room, observing the activity. At night, the place settings were rearranged, napkins moved about and silverware stacked or completely removed. The employees denied responsibility, and someone suggested that they had some spooky extra help in the dining room.

Occasionally, an extra waitress, who bears a striking resemblance to one who worked there in the early 1900s, appears in the dining room after closing. She checks the tables and the place settings and arranges cups and saucers. This mysterious waitress was spotted by a guest, who was admiring an elaborate, antique cabinet in the lobby. Glancing in its mirror, she was startled to catch a sudden reflection of a young woman standing behind her. She whirled around, but the lobby was empty.

It's believed that ghostly Ed Sackett keeps an eye on activities throughout the hotel. Many guests have heard unexplained footsteps in the halls late at night, and their closed windows are often reopened by invisible hands. Other times, open windows are suddenly slammed shut when no one is near. Fresh towels are left on the dressers in guest rooms by housekeepers, but they are often moved and lined up on the beds in orderly rows.

Ed Sackett is sometimes joined on his rounds by a lady in a flowing, gray skirt and a starched, white blouse with long, puffy sleeves. One evening, a guest encountered this woman in the hall, and as she walked past, the lady slowly vanished. Was Violet Sackett checking to be sure everything was going smoothly?

Over the centuries, the Jeffery children romped and played throughout the hotel. Guests have complained about children laughing and giggling and even knocking on room walls. Occasionally, there's the sound of a ball rolling across the floor in Room #3. The great-grandson of John Muir stayed overnight in Room #1. The next morning, he said that he'd been awakened by youngsters running up and down the hall, playing during the night. These juvenile disturbances always happen when the hotel has no young guests registered.

Rooms #22 and #8 often have unseen guests, and doors open and close mysteriously as dark shadows come and go. Lights flicker on and off, and there are whispers in the hall. When the door is quickly jerked open—surprise—no one's there. A group of California mediums and paranormal investigators had an unusual encounter in Room #8. While relaxing in the room after dinner, one woman felt something touch her, while another felt an unseen presence brush by. There was a sudden, cold draft in the room, which everyone noticed. Certain that they had unseen company, one medium asked the entity to demonstrate its presence by opening the room door from outside in the hall. The group waited quietly with their eyes fixed on the door. After a few minutes, it slowly opened by itself. There was no one in the hall. This phenomenon was captured on video and can be viewed on the Internet.

The Hotel Jeffery was recently purchased by Sarah Zahn and Forrest Monk, who have refurbished it. During the renovations, they lived in Room #8 and noticed their three cats acting strangely. They weren't too concerned, until the felines started waking them with loud growling and hissing, and Sarah described the normally calm kitties as looking like fuzzy porcupines. Their hair was standing straight up as they glowered and spit at something only they could see in one corner of the room. This racket and uproar became a nightly occurrence until the couple moved into their new quarters. Once out of Room #8, the fearful felines reverted to their usual calm demeanor.

While staying in Rooms #8 and #9, a family was watching a movie when the wife noticed the door handle turning as if someone in the hall was trying to enter. The door was locked, and looking through the peephole, she saw a woman wearing a 1880s gown and a nurse's cap. The woman was dabbing the forehead of an older man, who appeared ill and was leaning against her. When the guest's husband looked through the peephole, no one was there. When they opened the door, the hall was empty. What happened to the nurse and her patient?

Pets are welcome at the Jeffery, but some normally calm, well-behaved dogs seem frightened or bark uncontrollably at something their owners can't see. Forrest's brother helped with the renovations and stayed in Room #6 with his dog. He spent some restless nights, often awakened by frantic barking. His dog was always upset, growling, snarling and focusing on a corner of the room. One night, after an especially rough day, he was exhausted and didn't wake up when the dog started barking. The next morning he was shocked to see a large red mark on his cheek that he described as looking "like I'd been punched in the face." Then he recalled that he'd felt "a burning sensation" on his face sometime during the night but hadn't completely awakened.

One guest, who swears that he'll never spend another night at the Jeffery, complained that he heard voices and loud whispers "right next to me" when he was trying to sleep in Room #6. He complained about the disturbance, then laughed a bit sheepishly, admitting that he was really too scared to sleep.

Another Room #6 guest complained that he had been awakened several times during the night by "loud people running in the hall." There was no explanation for the noise, but maybe one of the hotel's more illustrious guests was stirring about. Thomas Edison, Ralph Waldo Emerson, John Wayne and Mark Twain all dropped by and spent the night at the Jeffery. Teddy Roosevelt stopped here when he was en route to Yosemite in 1903.

During the hotel renovations, new carpet was installed throughout the building. When the old floor covering was pulled up in Room #20, Sarah said the installers were surprised to find "blood spatter throughout the room on the floor." She said there was no blood on the old carpet, which she described as looking like it had been there for decades. So when was that old carpet laid down over these bloodstains? Whose blood was it, and what had happened in Room #20?

In September 2012, repairs were being made on the nearby highway, and three women in the road construction crew stayed over at the hotel. One was assigned Room #19, and the other two had Rooms #15 and #16. During the night, the lady in Room #19 awoke to see the door standing wide open. She got up, closed the door and returned to bed, only to have her blanket and sheet pulled off. Frightened, she joined the woman in Room #15. As soon as she entered the room, all the doors on the second floor slammed shut, one right after another. They were the only people in the hotel, and there were no open windows or unexplained drafts, so what made the doors slam?

One night, Sarah worked in the office until two o'clock in the morning and then made her rounds, checking the locked doors before going to her quarters. Early the next morning, when she came in to unlock and let the cook in, there was an antique cello sitting directly in her path. It had been moved about twenty feet from its place near the old piano. No one was in the hotel during the night, and the doors were locked. So who moved this antique instrument?

Sarah said she is uncomfortable in the Cedar Room, which is used for special events like wedding receptions, dances and meetings. "The room gives me the creeps. I won't go in by myself if the lights are off," she explained. Footsteps have been heard in this room when the hotel has been empty and she and Forrest were totally alone. Sometimes the sounds are coming from overhead, but there is no floor above the Cedar Room, just a steep, pitched roof.

A large group of Sacramento-based paranormal investigators, equipped with plenty of ghost hunting meters, recorders, cameras and sensitive equipment, held a séance in the Cedar Room. They recorded the faint sound of a man's voice, and several people caught glimpses of a shadowy figure in a corner of the room. One man said he felt like something had scratched him, and when his back was examined, everyone was startled to see several faint scratches.

When this group visited the restaurant and kitchen, several employees shared their paranormal experiences. A lone kitchen worker, sweeping the floor, said he was suddenly hit in the head by a box of cereal that had actually sailed across the room, as if it had been thrown.

When the evening cook was closing the kitchen for the night, he turned off the gas stove only to have the burners suddenly re-light. He turned off

The building of the Jeffrey Hotel contains walls of the original adobe structure that once housed a fandango hall. *Wendy Williams.*

the stove again, and the same thing happened. After checking for a leak, he turned the stove off for the third time, with the same results. It was some time before this exasperated cook was able to persuade the gas stove to remain turned off so that he could head home.

These paranormal investigators spent the night at the Jeffery, and two women requested Room #22. Aware of its activity, they scanned it with their meters and immediately obtained high EVP readings. One woman sensed a presence, which made her quite uncomfortable, and when the other asked, "Is someone here with us?" they received a clear answer: "Yes!" They captured this voice response on tape, but further questions went unanswered. They did not experience any other ghostly activity in the room, but many others have had strange experiences.

Occasionally, guests in Room #22 have been joined by a shadowy-looking man and a younger woman. This romantic duo floats through the door, embraces and, arms entwined, leisurely wanders about the room. Then the couple returns to the hall and slowly fades away.

In the fall of 2012, a guest went to sleep in Room #22 but awoke in the middle of the night absolutely terrified. He'd felt something tight around his neck like he was being strangled, and he had difficulty getting his breath. The frightened man had a restless night, and the next morning, he learned that a young woman had committed suicide in this room. She'd been abandoned by her lover and, seeing only a bleak future ahead, decided to end it all by hanging herself from the ceiling light fixture.

A photographer took a series of pictures in Room #22 and the adjacent rooms and got quite a surprise when he reviewed the results. He had captured an image of a shadowy figure, which moved from Room #20 to #21 in his photos. The image was not the photographer's shadow, and when he took the pictures, no one else was present.

No matter which room you rent, when you check into the Jeffery Hotel, you may be alone, but when you get settled, don't be surprised if you have some company. In #10, a woman dressed in a long white gown is often seen walking across the room to take a seat in the rocking chair. She rocks leisurely for a bit and then suddenly vanishes. Other guests have seen this same rocking chair slowly moving back and forth, but they are unable to see anyone seated in it.

Another group of California paranormal investigators spent three days and nights in the hotel and came away convinced that it's definitely home to several unknown entities. Equipped with every device known to modern ghost hunters, they picked up clear evidence of paranormal activity. This was closely aligned with the numerous eyewitness reports of unexplained events, and the group concluded that the Hotel Jeffery is home to at least seventeen different spirits. They said there are maids, a few distinguished-looking middle-aged women and several well-dressed gents, as well as a working girl or two and plenty of children. These investigators said emphatically that there was also a great deal of ghostly activity in the Magnolia Saloon and the hotel's dining room. Is it any wonder that, after spending so many years in this old hotel, some of these folks might be reluctant to move on?

When you step through the door from the hotel into the Magnolia Saloon, you're taking a giant step back through the centuries. This is one of the oldest watering holes in the Gold Country, and it's been in continuous operation since 1899, having been rebuilt after Coulterville's last disastrous fire. The Magnolia is a venerable old survivor and drifters, cowboys, bankers, the rich and resolute and the down at the heels have passed through its doors. History has come and gone, and the Magnolia has seen it all.

Its sturdy plank floor is worn and pitted from miners' boots, cowboys' spurs and the stiletto heels of the saloon girls. This old place saw many business deals finalized with a handshake and a drink. It has witnessed its share of brawls and boisterous celebrations, and plenty of gold dust and golden coins have slid across its old wooden bar. Towels once hung along the front of this ancient, hand-polished piece of the past so whiskered patrons could mop the suds from their handlebar moustaches and long beards.

The Magnolia Saloon is a living museum, full of old photos, relics and souvenirs of the days and the folks that are long gone. Its photographs are a veritable gallery of "Who's Who" and "Who Was" in Coulterville. Reminiscent of the past, it's no surprise that folks who once enjoyed this old place continue to hang around. There are numerous reports of an older man who stakes out the bar stool on the far end. He has his suds and watches the happenings around him and then suddenly disappears, leaving his empty mug.

Patrons of the Magnolia sometimes detect a whiff of cigar smoke, even though no one is smoking, and a bit of perfume drifts by on someone unseen. Paranormal experts say the spirits that remain behind in the Magnolia Saloon and the Jeffery Hotel seem to be fairly content. They have many tasks to handle, but the gentlemen don't forget to take time to enjoy a relaxing happy hour in this old saloon. As gnarled and ancient as the wisteria vine wrapped around the building, the Jeffery Hotel and its Magnolia Saloon are testimony to stubborn durability and man's need for conviviality and comfort.

BIBLIOGRAPHY

Abeloe, William. *Historic Spots in California*. Stanford, CA: Stanford University Press, 1948.

Browne, Juanita. *Nuggets of Nevada County History*. Nevada City, CA: Nevada County Historical Society, 1983.

Buck, Marcia, and Patricia Smith. *Gold Rush Nuggets*. Pasadena, CA: Castle Ventures, 1984.

Crain, Jim. *Historic Country Inns of California*. San Francisco, CA: Chronicle Books, 1977.

Devey, Davis. *History of Coulterville*. Coulterville, CA: Northern Mariposa County History Center, 1978.

Dwyer, Jeff. *Ghost Hunter's Guide to California's Gold Rush Country*. Gretna, LA: Pelican Press, 2009.

Garcez, Antonio. *Ghost Stories of California's Gold Rush Country and Yosemite National Park*. Hanover, NM: Red Rabbit Press, 2004.

Killeen, Jacqueline. *Country Inns of the Far West: California*. San Francisco, CA: 101 Productions, 1987.

Marston, Anna. *Records of a California Family*. San Diego, CA: Donald I. Segerstrom Memorial Fund, 1974.

Schlichtmann, Margaret. *The Big Oak Flat Road*. Fredericksburg, TX: Awani Press, 1986.

INTERNET RESOURCES

http://www.biography.com/haunted-history/episodes/hotels.
http://www.travelchannel.com/tv-shows/ghost-adventures.

HOTEL WEBSITES

American River Inn, Georgetown. http://www.americanriverinn.com/Home.html.
Cary House, Placerville. http://www.caryhouse.com/.
City and Fallon Hotels, Columbia. http://yosemitegoldcountry.com/lodging/columbia-city-fallon.
Dorrington Hotel, Dorrington. http://www.dorringtonhotel.com/.
Gunn House, Sonora. http://www.gunnhousehotel.com/.
Groveland Hotel, Groveland. http://www.groveland.com/.
Holbrooke Hotel, Grass Valley. http://holbrooke.com/.
Hotel Charlotte, Groveland. http://www.hotelcharlotte.com/.
Hotel Jeffery, Coulterville. http://www.hoteljeffery.com/.
Hotel Leger, Mokelumne Hill. http://www.hotelleger.com/.
Imperial Hotel, Amador City. http://www.imperialamador.com/.
Ione Hotel, Ione. http://www.ionehotel.com/.
Murphys Hotel, Murphys. http://www.murphyshotel.com/
National Hotel, Jackson. http://www.nationalhoteljackson.com/.
National Hotel, Jamestown. http://www.national-hotel.com/.
National Hotel, Nevada City. http://www.downtownnevadacity.com/pages/stay.html.
Nevada City Hotels. http://www.nevadacitychamber.com/c/biz/hotels-inns/.
Sierra Nevada House, Coloma. http://www.sierranevadahouse.com/.
Sonora Inn, Sonora. http://www.thesonorainn.com/.
St. George Hotel, Volcano. http://www.stgeorgevolcano.com/.

PARANORMAL GROUPS WEBSITES

American Paranormal Investigations. www.ap-investigations.com.
Atlantic Paranormal Society (TAPS). www.the-atlantic-paranormal-society.com.

Bay Area Ghost Hunters. www.meetup.com/Bay-Area_Ghost-Hunters/.
California Ghost Hunters. www.californiaghosthunters.net.
California Haunts Paranormal Researchers. www.californiahaunts.org.
Central California Paranormal Investigators. www.ccpi.org.
El Dorado Paranormal Investigations. www.edparanormal.com.
Ghost Trackers. www.ghost-trackers.org.
Haunted Paranormal Investigators. www.hpiparanormal.net.
Haunting America. www.hauntingamerica.com.
International Society for Paranormal Research. www.ispr.net.
The Shadowlands—Haunted Places. www.theshadowlands.net/places/.
Western Region Paranormal Research. www.wrpr-online.com.
Your Ghost Stories. www.yourghoststories.com.

ABOUT THE AUTHOR

Author Nancy Williams near her home in Evergreen, Colorado. *Tom Williams.*

Exploring adobe forts and Anasazi ruins in Arizona as a kid whetted Nancy's interest in western history. Moving to California's Gold Country was an opportunity to investigate a fascinating region and its colorful past. Her first magazine article was about a haunted Mother Lode hotel, and it was followed by others about the Gold Country. After thirty-one years in the Golden State, she moved to Colorado, with its high mountain vistas and abandoned mining camps, remnants of later gold and silver rushes. Bouncing over rocky ledges and around narrow precipices on a challenging Jeep trail was a new thrill. Nancy says completing this book was as challenging as climbing a "Fourteener" (a peak of fourteen thousand feet or higher).

Visit us at
www.historypress.net
....
This title is also available as an e-book